The Fall of France

The Fall of France

France MAY - JUNE 1940

Robert Jackson

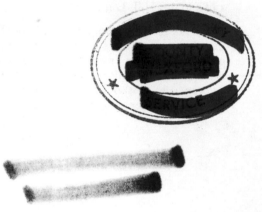

ARTHUR BARKER LIMITED
London
A Subsidiary of Weidenfeld (Publishers) Limited

Copyright © Robert Jackson 1975

Published in Great Britain by Arthur Barker Limited
11 St John's Hill, London SW11

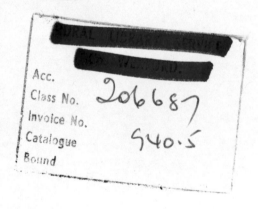
ISBN 0 213 16557 0

Printed in Great Britain by
Bristol Typesetting Co. Ltd
Barton Manor, Bristol

Contents

List of Illustrations   vi

List of Maps   vii

Acknowledgement   viii

Introduction   ix

1 Prelude to Disaster   1

2 Belgium and Holland, 10-15 May   40

3 The Ardennes and Northern France, 10-16 May   64

4 The Collapse in the North, 16-21 May   86

5 The British Expeditionary Force: The Road to Dunkirk   107

6 The Last Offensive   136

7 Battle in the Alps   148

Epilogue   155

Appendix 1   158

Appendix 2   161

Appendix 3   164

Maps   168

Bibliography   173

Index   175

Maps

(ON PAGES 168–72)

1 Disposition of Anglo-French armies on 9 May 1940
2 The Allied advance into Belgium, 10–12 May 1940
3 *Sichelschnitt* (modified Manstein Plan), implemented 10 May 1940
4 Encirclement of the northern armies
5 German breakthrough on the Somme and Aisne and French army dispositions on 12 June 1940

Maps drawn by Adrienne Kapadia

Illustrations

(BETWEEN PAGES 86 AND 87)

1 The BEF marching through Paris *(Radio Times Hulton Picture Library)*
2 Destroyed German tank *(Imperial War Museum)*
3 General Weygand *(Radio Times Hulton Picture Library)*
4 General Guderian *(Radio Times Hulton Picture Library)*
5 British Bristol Blenheims *(Imperial War Museum)*
6 German Stukas *(Imperial War Museum)*
7 Belgian church damaged by bombs *(Imperial War Museum)*
8 Belgian refugee *(Imperial War Museum)*
9 Tired men of the BEF return to England *(Imperial War Museum)*
10 Evacuated British troops look back at the burning Cherbourg supply dumps *(Imperial War Museum)*
11 Bodies and a gun abandoned in the Allied retreat *(Imperial War Museum)*
12 One of the first German pictures taken in Dunkirk *(Imperial War Museum)*
13 British and French prisoners at Dunkirk *(Imperial War Museum)*
14 German troops parade through the Arc de Triomphe *(Imperial War Museum)*

Acknowledgement

I have been indebted to many individuals for their help in preparing this book, but I should like in particular to mention Colonel John Forbes, Regimental Secretary of the Green Howards, whose assistance in preparing the account of the activities of 'Frankforce' proved invaluable, and by whose permission the extract from the September 1940 edition of the *Green Howards Gazette* appears on pages 127–31.

Introduction

Three and a half decades ago, Western Europe was the scene
of one of the most effective and devastating campaigns in the
history of warfare – a campaign whose lessons, in many
respects, still hold good today.

The political background to the Fall of France has been set
out in detail many times, and has often tended to overshadow
the events of the military campaign as a whole. It is therefore
the latter that forms the content of this book; those who
wish to delve deeply into the political aspects should refer to
the list of many first-class works in the bibliography, and it is
as a purely military history that this work should be read.

CHAPTER I

Prelude to Disaster

It was 08.00 hours on 10 January 1940, and Major Hellmuth Reinberger was far from happy. It was bitterly cold in the cockpit of the little Messerschmitt 108 communications aircraft, and to make matters worse Reinberger had a splitting headache – the result of a little too much conviviality in the Luftwaffe officers' mess at Münster-Loddenheide airfield the night before.

By rights, Reinberger should not have been flying today at all. After a pleasant evening at Loddenheide, he had intended to return to Münster – where he was paratroop liaison officer at the headquarters of Luftflotte 2 – and then catch an early morning train to Cologne, where he had to attend a staff conference.

It was Loddenheide's station commander, a Reserve Major named Erich Hönmanns, who had suggested that Reinberger should fly to Cologne instead of undergoing a dreary train journey. Hönmanns himself would do the piloting; he had flown during the First World War, still held a current private pilot's licence and was checked out on the Me 108. Taking Reinberger along without the proper authorization would mean bending a few regulations, but then who would ever know about the trip?

So it was that Reinberger found himself shivering in the 108's vibrating cockpit as the aircraft climbed away into the freezing cold of a January dawn. The weather was clear enough, with hardly a cloud in the sky and a flight visibility of over two and a half miles despite a ground mist; nevertheless, Reinberger was suddenly conscious of the risk he ran if anything should go wrong. Instinctively, his hands tightened on

the yellow pigskin briefcase that lay on his knees – the briefcase that carried a series of dossiers marked '*Streng Geheim*'
('Top Secret'). Their contents held the destinies of half a dozen
nations and thousands of men – Germans, Belgians, Dutch,
French and English. They were nothing less than the blueprint
for the proposed German offensive in the West.

On 15 March 1939, in defiance of the tenuous agreement
reached between Britain, France and Germany at Munich a
few months earlier, German troops marched into Prague and
added Czechoslovakia to the tentacular growth of Hitler's
Reich. It was the third spectacular and blatant *coup* pulled off
by the Germans in three years; the first had come on 7 March
1936, when the Wehrmacht, tearing to shreds the appropriate
clauses of the Versailles and Locarno Treaties, had occupied
the Rhineland; the second had occurred in March 1938, with
the annexing of Austria.

As Hitler had shrewdly anticipated, the occupation of
the Rhineland in 1936 had thrown the French Government –
steeped as it was in domestic trouble – into complete confusion. Since the German military effort involved not much
more than a single division, several leading French ministers –
including Monsieur Sarraut, the then Prime Minister – were in
favour of armed resistance, and it was true that at that time
the military advantage lay with France, on paper at least; she
could theoretically mobilize over half a million men within a
week, outnumbering the Germans by two to one. Technolog-
ically, Germany was better equipped to wage modern warfare,
but it would take her some time to bring all her resources into
play.

Still thinking in terms of a military counter-operation, the
French approached both the British and Belgians in an effort
to enlist their open support. The reaction of London and
Brussels, however, was cool, and within forty-eight hours it
was clear that if France was going to act, it would have to be
alone. Yet France's whole military planning was geared to the
defensive rather than the offensive, and it was now that the

serious gaps in the tactical structure of the French Army became glaringly apparent. Without full mobilization, French
military action in the Rhineland could be accomplished only
by forming new units from forces already *in situ* on the frontier, a course which would seriously weaken the defensive
system and was therefore full of risk; on the other hand, mobilization could be countenanced only if full-scale war was
planned. And that, in the spring of 1936, could not be considered.

The French Government was consequently left with no
alternative but to back down. Hitler's gigantic bluff – for such
it was – had worked, and his first military victory had been
achieved without a shot being fired.

His next victory – the *Anschluss* with Austria – was of even
greater strategic significance. At one stroke, France was now
confronted with a Third Reich of seventy-six million people
against her own forty-two million; still more serious, the union
with Austria completely neutralized the main border defences
of France's principal east European ally, Czechoslovakia, for
the latter's military planners had not thought it necessary to
create permanent fortifications along the Czech-Austrian frontier.

Despite the open threat to Czechoslovakia, France – whose
military alliance with that country dated back to January 1924
– did nothing except place her frontier forces on temporary
alert, and yet it was apparent to all except the blindest of
French politicians that the *Anschluss* must have given impetus
to any German plan for an invasion of Czechoslovakia. Such a
plan – code-named ' *Fall Grün* ' ('Plan Green') and drawn up
by Field Marshal von Blomberg – had in fact been in existence
since June 1937, and in November of that year Hitler had informed his General Staff that they should be ready to implement it ' as early as 1938 '.

Of all European nations, Czechoslovakia – created out of the
treaties that followed the First World War – was for Germany
the symbol of humiliation and defeat. Since its foundation in
1918, it had developed into the most forward-looking and

prosperous state in central Europe, even though its make-up of several different nationalities gave rise to serious domestic problems which, in 1937, were far from being solved. The population of Czechoslovakia included one million Hungarians, half a million Ruthenians and three and a quarter million Sudeten Germans, all of whom held far stronger ties with their mother countries than with the State of their domicile and who felt that the Czech Government had not honoured the promises made at the Paris Peace Conference in 1919 to the effect that the minorities be allowed a measure of autonomy. Internal political intrigue began to reach the danger level in 1933, when the Nazis came to power in Germany and infected the Sudeten Germans with the germ of nationalism; it led to the foundation of the Nazi-orientated Sudeten German Party, which was secretly financed by the German Foreign Office. By the beginning of 1938, the members of the Party, which included the vast majority of Sudeten Germans, were Adolf Hitler's almost to a man.

In March 1938, on Hitler's orders, the Sudeten German Party began to make demands on the Czech Government which were totally unacceptable to the latter. Both France and Britain at this stage failed entirely to grasp the real significance behind this move, which was to undermine the authority of the central government and provide a pretext for eventual German intervention. In fact, both London and Paris went out of their way to advise the Czech Government to provide concessions for the Sudeten Germans, being apparently convinced that Hitler wanted only justice for them. The German propaganda machine had done its work well.

In May, however, the situation changed dramatically. The principal cause was a major German security leak, picked up by British and French Intelligence, which indicated that the Germans were about to launch an attack on Czechoslovakia. Europe was immediately plunged into crisis; the Czechs began to mobilize, and for once Britain, France and Soviet Union showed signs of making a firm stand against the threat. The tension increased with a report – which later turned out to be false – that the Wehrmacht was massing its divisions in Saxony for a drive against the Czechs; diplomatic exchanges reached fever pitch, while in the background Dr Goebbels's Propaganda Ministry stepped up its wild stories of Czech atrocities against the Sudeten Germans.

The diplomatic activity during what was to become known as the May Crisis left the Germans in no doubt that France was prepared to go to the aid of Czechoslovakia in the event of war. The attitude of Chamberlain's government in Britain, however, was very different; there was no firm commitment to support the Czechs from this direction, only a vague threat that 'in the event of a European conflict, it was impossible to foresee whether Britain would not be drawn into it'.

To Hitler, such an attitude could be interpreted only as a sign of weakness. As history has since shown, it is more than probable that if Britain had joined France in taking a firm stand against Germany's aggressive intentions at this time, Hitler would not have embarked on the path of escalation that was to plunge the world once more into total war.

As it was, on 28 May Hitler called a meeting of the General Staff and ordered preparations to be made for an attack on Czechoslovakia by 2 October 1938, with a planned mobilization of ninety-six divisions and an immediate strengthening of Germany's western frontier. The new directive for *Fall Grün* caused immediate consternation among several of Hitler's senior generals, who, unlike the Führer, were not convinced that Britain and France would not be prepared to risk all-out war in the event of an assault on Czechoslovakia. Their concern, in fact, was great enough to give birth to the nucleus of a conspiracy against Hitler, with Generals Halder and Beck as its prime movers. Halder secretly arranged with the Oberkommando der Wehrmacht that he be given at least forty-eight hours' notice of an impending attack – a critical two days in which he would attempt to overthrow Hitler and withdraw the world from the brink of war.

This time, however, it was Hitler and not his generals who was right. As the summer of 1938 wore on, it became increasingly apparent that Britain, at least, was prepared to follow a policy of appeasement. In August, Chamberlain sent a special emissary – Lord Runciman – to Czechoslovakia with the somewhat dubious mission of acting as mediator between the Sudeten Germans and Prague; his attitude towards the former was conciliatory, and he urged the Czech Government to grant them their demands. To the Czech administration, it was plain that Runciman's real task was to pave the way for the handing over of the Sudetenland to Germany.

Meanwhile, in Berlin, final plans for the invasion were being drawn up; the deadline now was 1 October. It was at this juncture that Chamberlain, on 28 August, began to make secret moves to establish a personal contact between himself and Hitler in the hope of averting war. On 13 September, following a series of inflammatory speeches against Czechoslovakia during a Nazi Party rally in Nuremberg, Chamberlain sent the following message to the Führer : 'In view of the increasingly critical situation, I propose to come over at once to see you with a view to trying to find a peaceful solution. I propose to come across by air and am ready to start tomorrow. Please indicate earliest time at which you can see me and suggest place of meeting. I should be grateful for a very early reply.'

The meeting was held at Berchtesgaden, Hitler's mountain retreat, on 15 September. Hitler, fully conscious now that he held all the cards, was unswerving in his intention to solve the Sudeten question by force, if necessary. After some discussion, the tired British premier stated that although he recognized the principle behind the detachment of the Sudeten areas from Czechoslovakia, he could not commit himself until he had consulted his Cabinet and the French Government. For Hitler, it was a major tactical victory; from now on, in his dealings with Britain and France, he would allow no political consideration to limit his demands.

On 18 September Premier Daladier of France and his Foreign Minister, Georges Bonnet, arrived in London for talks on the Sudeten problem with the British Government. The Czechs themselves were not consulted. During the meeting the British and French agreed on the following proposals: all territories where Sudeten Germans formed more than fifty per cent of the population were to be turned over to Germany, in return for which Britain and France would guarantee the security of Czechoslovakia's new boundaries. This guarantee would replace the mutual assistance pact which Czechoslovakia already had with France.

These proposals were presented to the Czechs on 19 September; not surprisingly, they were rejected. Then began the betrayal; the following day, both Britain and France warned the Czechs that if they persisted in their rejection, the two big powers would no longer interest themselves in the fate of Czechoslovakia. Finally, on the 21st, with a bitter sense of betrayal, the Czech Government realized that it had no alternative other than to accept the Anglo-French plan.

The next day, at the little town of Godesberg, on the Rhine, Chamberlain had another meeting with Hitler during which the British Prime Minister gave lengthy details of the proposals made to Czechoslovakia and their reluctant acceptance by the Czech Government. To Chamberlain's amazement and anger, Hitler told him that the proposals were not acceptable to Germany. Nothing less than the complete occupation of the Sudeten areas by German forces would satisfy the Führer. The Czechs were to complete their evacuation of the Sudetenland by 28 September at the latest.

The argument continued, often furiously, for forty-eight hours. In the middle of it, Hitler was handed a report which stated that the Czechs had ordered full mobilization. For Chamberlain, it was almost the final blow. He knew now beyond all doubt that the Czechs were prepared to fight, and if that happened, it was hard to see how Britain and France could avoid being dragged into the ensuing conflict. All that was left for him to do was to try to persuade the British Cabinet to accept the latest Nazi demands, and to dissuade the French Government from taking any precipitate action. He failed, however, on both counts. Leading members of his

Cabinet opposed him, and on the 24th, the day of his return
to England, the French rejected the Godesberg proposals and
ordered partial mobilization of their forces. Moreover, the
French Government affirmed that it would go to the assistance of Czechoslovakia if the latter were attacked, provided
that British support was assured.

There was no way out. With the utmost reluctance,
Chamberlain agreed to inform Hitler that Britain would stand
in support of France if the latter went to war with Germany
over Czechoslovakia. In one last desperate attempt to bring
Europe back from the brink of disaster, he wrote a personal
letter to Hitler, urging the Führer to agree to a meeting with
the Czechs – at which British representatives would be present
– to try to settle some peaceful means of handing over the
Sudeten territories. Hitler replied that he would agree to such
a meeting only if the Czechs recognized the Godesberg proposals and evacuated the disputed areas by 1 October. They
were given forty-eight hours to make up their minds.

Meanwhile, mobilization continued, and in Berlin more than
one general was far from happy over the prospect of war. At
noon on 27 September, Hitler ordered seven divisions of assault
troops to move up to the Czech frontier; they were to be ready
to go into action at dawn on 30 September. Five new divisions
were also mobilized in secrecy to bolster the defences on
Germany's western front. On the other side of the coin, the
Czechs alone had mobilized one million men, with a field army
of eight hundred thousand supported by five hundred tanks;
they therefore outnumbered the German forces on both fronts
by two to one, and their armies in the field – thanks to the
massive Skoda arms complex – were backed up by a military
technology second to none in central Europe. On the western
front the weight of the French Army increased the odds against
Germany to nearly eight to one, added to which was the news
that the British Fleet was mobilizing.

Even if fighting without allied support, it was probable that
the Czech Army could hold out for at least three months. She
could commit all her available forces to the battle, while

Germany on the other hand would be forced to retain large forces on other fronts. In the event of a general war, there was no doubt in the minds of several German generals – Beck and Halder in particular – that Germany would lose. This view was supported by the German Naval c-in-c, Admiral Raeder, who on the evening of 27 September appealed to Hitler to refrain from opening hostilities.

At about the same time, Neville Chamberlain told the British people in the course of a radio broadcast:

How horrible, fantastic, incredible it is that we should be digging trenches and trying on gas-masks here because of a quarrel in a far-away country between people of whom we know nothing! I would not hesitate to pay even a third visit to Germany, if I thought it would do any good. . . . I am myself a man of peace to the depths of my soul. Armed conflict between nations is a nightmare to me; but if I were convinced that any nation had made up its mind to dominate the world by fear of its force, I should feel that it must be resisted. Under such a domination, life for people who believe in liberty would not be worth living: but war is a fearful thing, and we must be very clear, before we embark on it, that it is really the great issues that are at stake.

Shortly after making this broadcast, Chamberlain received a reply to his earlier personal letter to Hitler. In it, the Führer stated that he was prepared to join in a guarantee of Czechoslovakia's new frontiers. It was a shred of hope, and with the German ultimatum due to expire at 2 pm the next day – 28 September – Chamberlain seized on it avidly. 'After reading your letter,' he wrote in a personal message to Hitler, 'I feel certain that you can get all essentials without war, and without delay. I am ready to come to Berlin myself at once to discuss arrangements for transfer with you and representatives of the Czech Government, together with representatives of France and Italy if you desire. I feel convinced that we could reach agreement in a week.'

It was indicative of the confusion – not to say panic – that reigned at this time that Chamberlain made no consultation with the French premier, Monsieur Daladier, before drafting his latest letter. Neither did Daladier consult with the British Prime Minister; on 27 September, in fact, the French were approaching the problem quite independently and had just instructed their ambassador in Berlin to extend further proposals regarding the area of the Sudetenland to be handed over. While the ambassador was with Hitler, a message arrived from Mussolini, advising Hitler to agree to a conference, with Italy participating.

In the afternoon of 28 September, Hitler accordingly sent messages to Chamberlain and Daladier, proposing a meeting on the following day. The venue was to be Munich.

The conference began at 12.45 pm on 29 September in the Führerhaus in Munich's Königsplatz. The Czechs, on Hitler's insistence, were excluded; their unhappy delegates were left to kick their heels in an adjoining room until 10 pm, when they were taken to see Chamberlain's adviser, Sir Horace Wilson. He told them, quite bluntly, that the delegates of the four powers had agreed on the immediate evacuation of the Sudeten areas by the Czechs, handing over a map on which the boundaries of the affected territory had been pencilled in. When the Czech representatives began to protest, Wilson cut them short and walked out.

Soon after 1 am on 30 September, Hitler, Chamberlain, Mussolini and Daladier formally signed the Munich Agreement, permitting the Wehrmacht to begin its march into Czechoslovakia on 1 October and to complete the occupation of the Sudetenland by the 10th. The Czechs submitted to the Agreement at 12.50 pm that same day 'under protest to the world'. In a radio broadcast that evening, General Sirovy, the Czech premier, told his people bitterly : 'We are abandoned. We stand alone.'

It was true; but for Czechoslovakia, the consequences of Munich were far more disastrous than Sirovy's words conveyed. Not only had the nation lost eleven thousand square miles of territory, together with 2,800,000 Sudetenlanders and eight hundred thousand Czechs; it had also lost its carefully-planned fortress line, one of the most formidable in Europe, and more than three-quarters of its raw materials. At a single stroke of the pen, Czechoslovakia had been shattered both physically and economically, its continued identity dependent on the will of the Third Reich.

Czechoslovakia was lost, but the fate of that unhappy country was no longer the concern of the Western powers. While a tremendous shudder of relief passed through France and Britain, while Chamberlain made his 'peace for our time' speech to an enthusiastic crowd on his return to London, one man alone seemed to sense the awesome danger that confronted Europe as a result of Munich. On 5 October, in a speech to the Commons, Winston Churchill stated : 'We have sustained a total and unmitigated defeat. . . . We are in the midst of a disaster of the first magnitude. The road down the Danube, the road to the Black Sea has been opened. . . . All the countries of Mittel Europa and the Danube Valley, one after another, will be drawn in the vast system of Nazi politics radiating from Berlin. . . . And do not suppose that this is the end. It is only the beginning.'

For France in particular, Munich was a disaster; it seems incredible that her politicians failed to realize, or chose to ignore, the immediate implications of the Agreement. Hitherto, France's whole defensive strategy had been based on a series of alliances with the smaller powers on the other flanks of Germany and Italy : Czechoslovakia, Poland, Rumania and Yugoslavia. The thinking behind this was dictated by the question of population; Germany had twice as many people as France, and therefore when fully mobilized she had the manpower resources to field an army twice as big. Only a multinational alliance could redress the balance, and Munich – which wrote off thirty-five highly-trained Czech divisions at one blow – had torn it apart. There were also psychological factors to be considered; after Munich, the confidence of France's remaining Eastern allies in her integrity was severely damaged. The only hope of maintaining stability now rested with Russia, which had a military alliance with both France and Czechoslovakia, but Russia had not been invited to Munich, and Stalin, rankling under the snub, was already preparing to reconsider his foreign policy and adopt a friendlier attitude towards Germany.

Indications of the thaw in Russia's attitude were communicated to Hitler by his envoys in Moscow on 3 October. A week later, the Führer set plans in motion to achieve what had been his objective all along: the liquidation of the remainder of Czechoslovakia.

It must be possible [he told his military leaders], to smash at any time the remainder of Czechoslovakia if her policy should become hostile towards Germany. The preparations to be made by the armed forces for this contingency will be considerably smaller in extent than those for 'Green'; they must, however, guarantee a considerably higher state of preparedness since planned mobilization measures have been dispensed with. The organization, order of battle and state of readiness of units earmarked for that purpose are in peacetime to be so arranged for a surprise assault that Czechoslovakia herself will be deprived of all possibility of organized resistance. The object is the swift occupation of Bohemia and Moravia and the cutting off of Slovakia.

It has often been said that when two nations which are potentially hostile to one another embark on an arms race, the result is inevitably war. This is far from the case. Almost every war in history has been born from the military strength of one nation against the weakness of another. Munich hammered this point home, and now, belatedly, Britain and France began to take notice of it. Both countries, faced with the threat of Nazi Germany, were already making determined efforts to shrug off the hangover caused by the drastic economic measures imposed on their defences during the early 1930s; France, as a first step, had extended her period of military service to two years in March 1935, and in September 1936 – six months after the Wehrmacht occupied the Rhineland – provision was made to create three light mechanized and two armoured divisions in an attempt to bring the French Army on to a mechanized footing.

Several months earlier, French Intelligence had advised the

government that the Germans were forming their first Panzer division, and although the French – with the possible exception of a number of forward-thinking army officers such as Charles de Gaulle – were slower than the Germans to realize the potential of the tank as an assault vehicle, they nevertheless made a laudable effort to retain a technological lead by producing the prototypes of several excellent armoured fighting vehicles. In 1935 the most modern tank available to the French Army was the small 11-ton D.1, equipped with one 47-mm gun and two machine-guns; a version with heavier armour, the D.2, entered service in 1937, but only one battalion was equipped with it. In the autumn of 1935, under the modernization programme initiated by General Maxime Weygand, the French Army C-in-C, several new armoured fighting vehicles (AFVs) were ordered into production; the first of these was the 12-ton Hotchkiss H.35 light tank, initially fitted with a 25-mm and later a 37-mm gun. Two hundred were ordered, together with three hundred Renault R.35 infantry support tanks. In addition there was the 20-ton Somua medium tank, designed as a private venture by the Societe d'Outillage Mécanique et d'Usinage d'Artillerie of St Ouen, a Schneider subsidiary. It was equipped with one 47-mm gun and one machine-gun.

Finally, there was the excellent B.1, a 33-ton monster with 60-mm armour plating and a 350-hp engine that gave it a top speed of 40 mph. Later described by the German Panzer General Heinz Guderian as the best tank in the field in 1940, it had a crew of five and was fitted with one 75-mm and one 47-mm gun and two machine-guns. During the campaign of May and June 1940, German anti-tank gunners found that their shells simply bounced off it. Its main disadvantages were that it was technically complex, which increased the risk of breakdown and made it unsuited to mass production; it used a large amount of fuel, which cut down its endurance to a little over five hours; and it was expensive, costing a million and a half francs per vehicle. Nevertheless, it was to form the mainstay of the French Armoured Divisions.

Production of the new AFVs, and indeed the whole rearma-

ment programme, progressed with painful slowness. Apart
from technical delays, the major factor was a political one;
the programme was initiated during the term of the unhappy
Third Republic, with its spate of successive governments which
made it impossible to adhere to any kind of consistent policy;
then in 1936 came the rise to power of the Popular Front,
obsessed by the futile dream of international disarmament and
attempts to solve France's industrial and labour problems by a
sweeping programme of nationalization. The latter was to hit
the armaments industry harder than the indecision of all the
previous governments combined, disrupting it badly at the
very time when its resources and considerable ingenuity were
most needed. The only good thing to come out of nationalization, in fact, was the sudden realization – which came as a
result of inspections by Government experts of the various
concerns being taken over – that the whole of France's vital
machine-tool industry was obsolete compared with that of
other industrial nations. Out of more than half a million
machines in service only twenty-five thousand were less than
ten years old; a similar number dated back to 1870 and even
earlier. The industry, moreover, had only ten thousand em-
ployees compared with seventy thousand in Germany.

Inter-departmental rivalries also contributed greatly to slow-
ing down the rearmament programme. Towards the end of
1935, for example, General Weygand managed to secure a
grant of four thousand million francs from the Ministry of
Finance, to be spread over a four-year period, but during the
year and a half that followed, two successive Ministers of War,
General Maurin and Colonel Fabry, both of them ex-gunners
who were quite inflexible in their outlook, insisted on a major
proportion of the available funds going to the artillery. There
was little or no co-operation at any level between different
army formations, and still less between the army and the arms
industry that served it. There was more than one instance of a
new piece of equipment being produced to some army specification, only to be rejected later because not enough thought had
gone into the specification in the first place.

Nowhere were the deficiencies more apparent than in the Armée de l'Air, the French Air Force, which in the mid-1930s was still regarded essentially as a tool of the army with no scope for independent action. By the middle of 1937, the nationalization programme of the Popular Front – which collapsed in June of that year – had reduced the French aircraft industry to a demoralized patchwork of small factories scattered throughout the country; there was only one factory equipped to undertake mass production.

In January 1938 a new and dynamic Air Minister, Guy La Chambre, assumed office; he was horrified by the obvious defects that confronted him. Conscious that he might already be too late, he did his best to salvage what he could from the wreckage. The following March, under his direction, a new construction programme was laid down, calling for the building of 2,500 modern combat aircraft at a rate of two hundred a month. In the light of the disorganized state of the aircraft industry, and taking into account the fact that the Armée de l'Air received only a quarter of the defence budget, the plan was far from realistic, and by the beginning of 1939 it was clear that the gap between French and German military aircraft production was growing steadily wider. The sole exception was fighter production; modern French fighter types were coming off the assembly line at a fast rate, and the combined British and French fighter strength was approaching parity with that of the Germans and Italians.

In bombers of all types, however, the Armée de l'Air was seriously deficient. The bomber force, in fact, was so obsolete that in September 1938 General Vuillemin, the French Chief of Air Staff, forbade its use except on night operations. For a force whose whole concept was based on tactical support of the army, it was astonishing that the potential of the dive-bomber, which in the German Luftwaffe was being developed as the very spearhead of a ground assault, appeared to have been completely ignored; the only such machines in French service were naval aircraft, and they numbered only a couple of squadrons.

Even Guy La Chambre's assessment of the position failed to take the dive-bomber's importance into account, and no aircraft of this type was included in the new bomber production order which totalled 876 machines. It was a hopelessly optimistic figure; right from the start, production was crippled by the aircraft industry's inability to mass-produce, and by August 1939 only 399 bombers were in service. Most of these were obsolete fixed-undercarriage types such as the Amiot 143; the only French medium bomber with a retractable undercarriage was the Bloch 210, which was outdated in every other respect, and the Liore et Olivier LeO 451. The latter was a sleek, modern type comparable with anything in Luftwaffe service, but in August 1939 only five had reached the French squadrons. In an attempt to fill the gap two American bomber types, the Martin 167 and the Douglas DB-7, were ordered early in 1939, but it would be over a year before the first deliveries took place. The overall seriousness of the situation was summed up by General Vuillemin, who in August 1939 wrote to Guy La Chambre:

The power of our bombing units has remained unchanged since September 1938 and is as restricted now as it was then. The poor performance of our bombers will necessitate very prudent operations during the first months of the war. The modern types built in France or awaited from abroad have not yet been delivered to the units. Therefore, the renovation of our offensive power will become effective only in four or five months' time.

Meanwhile, the international situation had once again taken a turn for the worse; on 15 March 1939, revealing the Munich Agreement for the worthless scrap of paper that it was, German forces flooded across the Czech border into Bohemia and Moravia. They met no resistance and by nightfall they had occupied Prague. The following day Slovakia too was taken over, and the nation of Czechoslovakia had ceased to exist. Protests from Britain and France were swept aside in the heady triumph of Hitler's 'march to the east'. There could be no turning back now; Germany was plunging unchecked down the road to war.

There remained France's alliance with Poland, dating back to 1921. Until March 1939 both France and Britain had believed that, after Czechoslovakia, Germany's next move would be against Rumania; now, with Slovakia as the jumping-off point, it appeared that the greatest threat was directed against Poland. At this point, belatedly, the British Government declared that it would lend the Polish Government all possible support if Poland were attacked and put up resistance. This unilateral declaration came as a bombshell to Hitler; in the light of all that had gone before, in view of everything that Chamberlain had sacrificed in the tenuous cause of peace, it seemed incomprehensible that the British Prime Minister should choose this time to make a stand, and particularly in favour of a country whose leadership had up to now been distinctly pro-German, to the extent of open collaboration in the dismembering of Czechoslovakia.

On 7 April the situation was further complicated by Italy's invasion of Albania. A week later, Britain and France extended their guarantees to cover Greece and Rumania. The sides that would be ranged against one another in the great conflict to come were beginning to take shape.

In June, Britain and France made a desperate bid to enlist Russian aid in guaranteeing the integrity of Poland. The talks dragged on for weeks and were a complete fiasco. The main Soviet negotiator, Marshal Voroshilov, asked the British delegation how many divisions Britain was prepared – or indeed able – to send to France on the outbreak of hostilities. The reply was: five infantry and one motorized. The Soviet Union, declared Voroshilov, could field 120 infantry and sixteen cavalry divisions, five thousand cannon and ten thousand armoured vehicles. The Marshal also pointed out that the Soviet Union had a 'complete military plan' for action in support of Poland, and asked for details of similar co-ordinated action on the part of France and Britain. The British and French delegates were forced to admit that no such plan existed.

In any case, the tripartite negotiations were largely of an academic nature, for the Polish Government had made it clear that under no circumstances would it allow the Red Army on to Polish soil; memories of the Russo-Polish war of 1920 were still too vivid. As the Polish leader Marshal Smigly-Ridz put it: 'With the Germans we risk losing our liberty. With the Russians we would lose our souls.'

Within a month, it became clear that Soviet participation in the talks had been an enormous bluff. Even before the talks ended, the German and Soviet Foreign Ministers – Ribbentrop and Molotov – were putting the finishing touches to the document that was to be the prelude to war: the Nazi-Soviet Non-Aggression Pact.

The British and French Governments learned of the signing of the pact on the afternoon of 23 August and both called emergency Cabinet meetings. The feelings of both powers were summed up by the French Minister for Foreign Affairs, Georges Bonnet, who stated:

The German-Russian Pact has totally altered the balance of power. Henceforth, Poland will no longer be able to look to the USSR for support, and – worse still – we may have to fear a German-Russian entente *against* Poland. Rumania, for her part, will be pressured into supplying Germany with all the raw materials she needs. . . . Turkey will not go to war unless there is a direct threat to her in the Balkans; England, on the other hand, will stand completely at our side, although she is only just beginning the rearmament of her land forces. On the intentions of the German Government, let us be under no illusions; they are not bluffing. They are resolved to take Danzig and the Polish Corridor, even though it should result in a general war.

Such are the facts. Now, the excuse given by the Soviet Union for breaking off negotiations with us is Warsaw's refusal to allow Russian troops passage across Polish territory. What must be our attitude? Should we adhere blindly to our alliance with Poland, or would it be better to push Warsaw towards a compromise? We should then at least gain time to increase our military strength and improve our diplomatic position. But a compromise would risk enfeebling the Franco-Polish alliance, essential as it is to the defence of France. . . .

That last sentence was, in a nutshell, the essence of the

whole dilemma. In August 1939 France had 120 divisions against the 200 that Germany could put into the field; the addition of Poland's 80 divisions was therefore essential to redress France's position of considerable numerical inferiority. To this total Britain would theoretically be able to add a further 40 divisions by the spring of 1940, and if Germany violated the neutrality of Holland and Belgium, that would bring another 30 divisions to the Allied side, making a grand total of 270. Everything, in fact, hinged on the ability of the Poles to hold the Germans until the onset of winter, preventing a further major offensive until the coming of spring; by that time the British should be in a position to land on the Continent in strength.

It was now that the full impact of the disastrous defensive strategy that had dominated French military thinking over the past two decades made itself felt. Now, too late, France's military leaders realized that their country was in no way equipped to take an effective part in a fast-moving, mobile war where campaigns would be decided by the dive-bomber and the tank. Yet it was the very fear of such a war, coupled with the vulnerability of her eastern frontier, that had led to the emphasis on a defensive strategy in the first place. In both 1870 and 1914 an enemy army, striking fast and hard, had flooded across the eastern frontier to the gates of Paris itself; and in the four deadly years that followed 1914, a million and a half Frenchmen had died in the mud and blood of the trenches to preserve what was left of France's 'sacred soil'.

In 1922, an Army Commission was appointed to look into France's existing defence policy and to make recommendations for the future. Led by Marshal Joffre, it visited the famous battlefield of Verdun, where a series of underground forts had defied a whole German Army Corps and the biggest concentration of artillery in history for ten months, and was suitably impressed; what might have been the outcome of the war, and the saving of life and territory, if France had possessed an interlocking web of such forts along the whole of her eastern frontier in 1914!

For the best part of a decade the Commission and successive governments argued over the feasibility of a fortified 'eastern wall' running the length of the frontier; one blueprint after another was studied only to be torn up. On two things only the military were agreed : the fortified front would have to be continuous – and it would cost an enormous sum of money to create. Finally, in January 1930, both chambers of the French National Assembly voted for work on the fortified line to begin immediately and set aside the vast sum of three thousand million francs, to be spread over four years, for its construction. The deadline for its completion was to be 1935, the year in which – under the terms of the Versailles Treaty – French forces of occupation were to be withdrawn from the Rhineland. The line was to extend from Basle on the Swiss border to Longwy, at the junction of the Belgian, Luxembourg and French frontiers. Its strongest points, covering a length of eighty-seven miles, were designed to protect Lower Alsace and the Metz-Nancy sector, both of which were particularly vulnerable to a large-scale thrust from the east. The line varied in depth, but at its strongest points it consisted of a series of anti-tank obstacles and barbed wire entanglements facing the frontier, supported by reinforced concrete blockhouses and pillboxes. Behind them was a deep anti-tank ditch, beyond which lay the line's network of underground casemates and forts. Each casemate, protected by up to ten feet of concrete, was equipped with quick-firing anti-tank guns, machine-guns and grenade-throwers; it had a garrison of twenty-five men whose living quarters were on a lower level.

Every three to five miles along the line, supporting the casemates, was a subterranean fort of concrete and steel. These forts were truly remarkable feats of engineering; the biggest, with a garrison of twelve hundred officers and men, consisted of eighteen blockhouses, each with a retractable turret housing guns ranging in calibre from 37-mm to 135-mm. There were powerful generators to supply the forts with heat and light, compressors to ensure a constant supply of fresh air, stores and ammunition magazines, the whole linked by a series of corri-

dors which were completely bombproof and up to a mile and a half long. In the larger forts, a miniature electric railway provided a rapid means of transport for personnel and material. Each fort was divided into two separate units, so that if one was knocked out, the other could continue to function independently, and the field of fire of each fort covered all neighbouring forts and casemates. Backing up the whole structure were mobile infantry units, with supporting artillery, who could be moved up rapidly to support the fort complexes in the event of enemy infiltration.

Work went ahead on the fortifications – known as the Maginot Line after André Maginot, the War Minister of the day – at a fast rate, and its eighty-seven miles of main defences were substantially completed by 1935. By this time the Line had already cost seven thousand million francs, far in excess of the budgeted figure, and the cost of maintaining it imposed an almost intolerable burden on a country whose economy was ailing – and one, moreover, where a strong Left Wing, opposed to rearmament in any form, made its voice continually heard. The result, inevitably, was that the French Army was compelled to suffer severe cuts in other fields, to such an extent that it became impossible, for reasons of finance, to carry out large-scale military manœuvres in 1936 and 1937.

Most serious of all, the Maginot Line remained at best only a partial shield against an attack from the east against metropolitan France. At its northern end there was no extension of the fortifications to cover the 250-mile common frontier between France and Belgium – and this despite the fact that in 1914 the German Army, following the brilliantly-devised Schlieffen Plan, had debouched into France across the drab Belgian plains. There were a number of reasons for this omission, apart from the question of cost. The first, and not the least important, was that an extension of the Line would have to pass right through the middle of the big industrial areas around Lille and Valenciennes, which would lead to unacceptable disruption; the second was that Belgium herself, separated from her French ally by a fortified line, might feel justified in adopting a policy of complete neutrality. In view of this, the French were prepared in Belgium's case to adopt an offensive posture – although it went very much against their overall defensive policy – by sending their forces across the border to fight a delaying battle on Belgian soil. This strategy was feasible enough in 1935, when the French Army still enjoyed considerable numerical superiority over the Wehrmacht; but by 1939 the Germans' Panzer tactics had made nonsense of it.

Between 1935 and 1939, then, while the Germans broke all records to develop their offensive capability, the French – like a tortoise retreating into its shell – retired behind the mythical impregnability of the Maginot Line, apparently oblivious to its glaring deficiencies; deficiencies which should have come to the fore when, in October 1936, King Leopold III of Belgium revoked his country's treaty with France and opted for a return to neutrality, leaving the French northern flank wide open.

There was another factor to be considered, too. In the Rhineland, the Germans had been proceeding at a fast rate with the construction of their own line of fortifications, the Siegfried Line. The presence of the Siegfried Line, protecting Germany's western frontier, meant that the Germans could transfer large numbers of troops from this area in relative safety from an attack by the French while they completed an offensive operation against Poland; once this had been achieved, the full weight of the Wehrmacht would be free to turn on France.

Despite all the shortcomings, the French Government in August 1939 saw no alternative other than to lend its full support to Poland should the latter be attacked. On 25 August Neville Chamberlain also reaffirmed Britain's intention to stand by her Polish ally. In both countries, final mobilization continued relatively smoothly; in France the call-up of reservists and men on leave had already begun on 21 August, and by nightfall on the 25th almost two million men were under arms, bringing a total of sixty-seven divisions on to a war footing. In addition, five divisions of the British Expeditionary Force, supported by an Air Component, were scheduled to land on the Continent during the next few days.

Meanwhile, the Germans had been mobilizing secretly and with great speed. By the 21st there were four divisions on the Polish frontier; on the 23rd the Poles began to mobilize, forty-eight hours before the German invasion was scheduled to begin. At 18.30 hours on 25 August the 1st and 4th Panzer Divisions, supported by fifteen hundred aircraft of Luftflotten 1 and 4, stood ready to spearhead the attack.

Then, suddenly, the whole programme was postponed for six days. Finally, after a week of tension, Hitler issued his War Directive No. 1 at 12.40 hours on 31 August; it ordered the assault to start at 04.45 on 1 September 1939.

Fifteen minutes before that time, a group of Junkers 87 dive-bombers of Stuka-Geschwader 1 attacked Polish positions near the strategic Dirschau bridge over the Vistula. Their 500-pound bombs sparked off the chain reaction that was to flame across the world for six years, annihilating fifty million people in its passing.

At eleven o'clock in the morning of 3 September, Britain, honouring her obligations to Poland, declared war on Germany. France followed suit a few hours later. In 1914, similar declarations had been accompanied by cheers and the throwing of flowers by wildly enthusiastic crowds in London and Paris; this time there was only sobriety, fear and a certain determination. The lost legions of 1914-18 still formed too tangible a spectre for the sentiment to be otherwise.

By the end of the second week in September, the French had succeeded in concentrating an impressive force on their north-eastern frontier. It comprised thirty-nine first-line infantry divisions, nine ' B ' divisions – consisting of reserve troops, most of them approaching middle age and seriously deficient in every kind of equipment – three cavalry divisions, two light armoured divisions and a miscellany of artillery regiments, machine-gun regiments and battalions. There were also seven fortress regiments, which were expanded to forty in number during the weeks following the outbreak of war.

In September 1939 the three French cavalry divisions were still mainly horsed, with two regiments of conventional cavalry supported by an armoured car regiment, an artillery regiment and a battalion of dismounted dragoons. In December, the three divisions were amalgamated and re-formed into five light cavalry divisions, each consisting of one horsed brigade and one mechanized.

The two light armoured divisions, the 2nd and 3rd, were also amalgamated and formed into a Cavalry Corps under General R. J. A. Prioux. Each division comprised a combat brigade equipped with Hotchkiss and Somua tanks, and a reconnaissance brigade of armoured cars, motor-cycles and one regiment of motorized dragoons. A third light armoured division was to form in the spring of 1940.

Because of delays in the production of the B.1 tank, it was not until January 1940 that the French were in a position to begin forming two heavy armoured divisions (Divisions Cuirassées), followed by a third in March. Each division comprised a combat brigade of two battalions with a total of sixty-two B.1 tanks, and two battalions of Hotchkiss with eighty-four fighting vehicles. Supporting infantry consisted of a battalion of motorized *chasseurs* per division, the whole being supported by an artillery regiment with twenty-four 105-mm guns and a battery of 47-mm anti-tank guns. Each division was supposed to have had a flight of army observation aircraft attached to it, but these never arrived.

In addition to these units, the various French field armies also had attached to them several battalions of light tanks: sixteen of Renault 35s, two of FCMS and one of Hotchkiss, each battalion having a strength of forty-five vehicles. Six more battalions were equipped with ancient Renault FTS of 1918 vintage, all of them so outdated as to be completely useless.

Completing the picture in the north and east were a wide variety of miscellaneous units; two battalions of light infantry from North Africa, two regiments of the Foreign Legion, the Garde Republicaine – and the Poles. The thousands of Poles who escaped when their country was overrun, or who were already in the west when the Germans attacked, formed two infantry divisions, the first of which was active by March 1940, while the Groupe de Chasse Polonaise – Polish Fighter Group – was to fight with distinction alongside the French Air Force.

The first week in September saw a rapid concentration of the French Army Group Two, comprising the Third, Fourth and Fifth Armies under the command of General A. G. Pretelat, along the Rhine between Strasbourg and Selestat. As early as 24 August, AG Two had been warned to stand by for a limited offensive in the Saar in the event of a German attack on Poland, and on 4 September General Gamelin, the French Commander-in-Chief Land Forces, ordered the assault to go ahead. Although the forces to be used in the operation were not yet fully assembled, the Fourth Army – led by the 11th 'Iron Division' – crossed the Rivers Blies and Sarre and advanced five miles under cover of darkness to within sight of Saarbrücken. At the same time, a force of Algerian infantry from the 4th North African Division, supported by a cavalry regiment, occupied a stretch of the Warndt Forest, while further to the east v Corps marched into the Ohrenthal Salient.

Within forty-eight hours, the French had succeeded in advancing along the whole of a twenty-five-mile front, although they had not reached the forward positions of the Siegfried Line. In London and Paris, newspapers hailed the offensive as a 'massive success' which had achieved 'overwhelming gains'. In fact, nothing could have been further from the truth. The Germans had resisted the offensive bitterly, and the French – advancing over carefully-laid minefields – had suffered heavy casualties. The only gains were a few villages which the enemy had for tactical reasons decided to abandon.

By 12 September, Gamelin had relinquished the idea of further offensive action in the Saar. It was unlikely to help the Poles, who were crumbling fast under the German onslaught; and within a few days the Germans would be in a position, following the transfer of forces from the east, to launch a counter-attack against the French, which would place the advance elements of the Third, Fourth and Fifth Armies in a dangerous position. The latter were therefore pulled back to the line of the Saar and Blies; in October the Germans attacked their forward positions and there was some fierce fighting, but with the approach of winter the front settled down to some kind of stability, with only the mounting of occasional offensive patrols to break the boredom.

Meanwhile, the French High Command had begun to lay plans to counter a possible German full-scale offensive in the west. The feeling was that, because of the difficulty that would be involved in forcing a passage through the Ardennes and the Maginot Line, a German thrust would come by way of Belgium – in much the same way as the German Army, following the famous invasion plan devised by Count von Schlieffen, had launched their assault on the Western Front in 1914.

At the end of September General Georges, commanding the French North-Eastern Army Zone, put forward a scheme, known as the Escaut Plan, whereby two armies, one French and one British, would advance into Belgium to face a German threat and form a defensive line along the Escaut River from the French frontier at Condé as far as Ghent. The plan depended, of course, on securing the Belgian Government's approval, and much of it hinged on the ability of the Belgian Army to extend the line and hold it from Ghent to Antwerp. In November, however, Allied Intelligence indicated that a German attack would also involve Holland. and since the Escaut Plan did not cover Dutch territory, it was abandoned in favour of a new scheme. Known as the Dyle Plan, this envisaged an Allied main line of resistance based on the River Dyle, which lay further to the east in Belgium and from which a rapid advance could be made into Holland. This plan, known also as Plan D, was formally approved by the Allied Supreme Council in London on 17 November.

In its finalized form, Plan D made provision for the Allied armies to occupy a continuous defensive line from the Dutch border to Mézières, in northern France. In the extreme north, the defence of Holland would rest with eight Dutch divisions; immediately to the south came the French Seventh Army, holding a line between Turnhout and Breda; then the Belgian Army, from Louvain to Antwerp; on the Belgians' right flank the British Expeditionary Force, lying between Wavre and Louvain and effecting a junction with the French First Army, in position between the BEF and Namur; and finally, between Namur and Mézières on the southern flank of the line, came the French Ninth Army.

The French and British armies whose task it would be to implement Plan D were grouped together under Army Group One, commanded by General Billotte. Because of the belief of General Gamelin and the High Command that a German attack would take the form of a 'right hook' through northern Belgium, ignoring the thickly-wooded Ardennes and the steep banks of the River Meuse, France's two best armies, the First and the Seventh were to be placed north of Namur, with the Belgians and the BEF between them. In September 1939, the British Expeditionary Force – commanded by Lord Gort – comprised two Army Corps of four divisions, concentrated between Amiens, St Pol and Vimy; it was not until October that General Sir Alan Brooke's II Corps moved up to take over the Lille sector along the Belgian frontier from the French 51st Division. II Corps was the BEF's left flank, with I Corps on its right and on the left General Fagalde's XVI Corps, forming part of the French Seventh Army under General Giraud. A fifth BEF Division, the 5th, under Major-General H. E. Franklyn, landed in France during December; it was followed by five territorial divisions – 48, 50, 51, 42 and 44, in that order – between January and April 1940.

The high standard of the Allied armies in the north contrasted sharply with the all too apparent deficiencies of General Huntziger's Second French Army to their south, holding the line of the Meuse in the Sedan area and the western end of the Maginot Line and joining up on its left with General Corap's Ninth Army. In this sector, sixteen poorly-equipped and poorly-

trained divisions, half of them ' B ' or second-class, had the task
of holding a ninety-five mile stretch of front where the fortifications were at best only partially complete.

To the right of the Second Army, which also formed part of
Billotte's Army Group One, was Army Group Two, whose
Third, Fouth and Fifth Armies – as mentioned earlier – had
undertaken the limited offensive on the Saar Front during the
first weeks of the war. Finally, on France's south-eastern frontier, came Army Group Three under General Besson, facing
the as yet neutral Italians across the Alps. It comprised the
Sixth Army – later to be redesignated the Army of the Alps –
with two Corps, XIV with its HQ at Lyon and XV at Marseille,
the whole mustering three active divisions of Alpine troops
and five reserve divisions. These forces had the task of defending three fortified sectors: the Alpes-Maritimes, Dauphiné and
Savoie, and the Rhône near the Swiss border. Later, when the
Italians showed signs of remaining passive, some of the active
divisions were transferred for tours of duty in the north; by
March 1940 Besson's Army Group consisted of the Eighth
Army and what remained of the Sixth, holding the Rhine from
Selestat to the Swiss border, while the force confronting the
Italians was whittled down to a single active division, the 2nd
Colonial, together with three Alpine reserve divisions and
seven fortress Demi-Brigades. High up in the mountains there
was also a thin line of outposts manned by highly skilled ski
reconnaissance troops (*chasseurs-éclaireurs*) whose task it would
ultimately be to contain an initial Italian thrust.

The French High Command, meanwhile, had been basically
correct in its assumption that the German invasion plan had
been drawn up along the lines of the classic Schlieffen Plan of
1914, involving a swing through Belgium to skirt the Maginot
defences and the natural obstacles of Meuse and Ardennes. On
19 October 1939, following the rapid German victory in Poland,
the German General Staff had drawn up the first draft of such
a plan, known as '*Fall Gelb*' ('Plan Yellow') for an assault in
the west. It stemmed from a directive issued by Hitler dated 9
October, calling for an immediate offensive in the west – an

idea that filled most of his generals with consternation. After the losses suffered in the Polish campaign, it would need considerable time before the Army and Luftwaffe were once again strong enough to embark on such a major undertaking. Both von Brauchitsch, the Army c-in-c, and Halder, his Chief of Staff, considered that a new offensive at this early date could result only in disaster. Nevertheless, Hitler was the Supreme Commander, and his orders had to be obeyed; the plan was consequently drawn up.

Fall Gelb differed from the earlier Schlieffen Plan in that, whereas the latter had envisaged a swing to the south after the initial thrust through Belgium in a manœuvre designed to trap the French armies against the Swiss frontier, *Gelb* would spear westwards to the Channel coast. Its primary objective was to secure central Belgium, inflicting as large a defeat as possible on the Allied forces in the process. Three army groups were to take part in it, driving through Holland, Belgium and the Ardennes; the most difficult task was likely to fall on Army Group B, commanded by General Fedor von Bock, which was to batter its way through Belgium to the Channel.

Army Group A, which was to drive through the Ardennes, was commanded by General von Rundstedt. His Chief of Staff, General Erich von Manstein, was not in favour of the plan as it stood. He believed that von Bock's Army Group would confront such strong Allied forces in Belgium that no decisive breakthrough would be achieved; it would be far better, in his opinion, for the main German assault to take place in the Ardennes, Army Group A's sector.

This belief was strengthened when the German Army's leading tank expert, General Heinz Guderian of XIX Panzer Corps, stated that a tank offensive through the tricky Ardennes terrain should be entirely possible with the proper planning, even though most of the generals in the Army High Command believed it would not, and had told Hitler so at an earlier conference.

The persistent Manstein, however, got nowhere, and the concept of *Fall Gelb* remained unchanged – with the exception

that, on Hitler's orders, a force of two armoured and one
motorized infantry divisions were to stand by 'to gain a surprise hold on the west bank of the Meuse by or south-east of
Sedan, thereby creating a favourable situation for subsequent
phases of the operation'. As for Manstein, he was eased quietly
out of the picture and posted to command an infantry corps
at Stettin, in East Prussia, where he would have no further
opportunity to make a nuisance of himself.

The original date for the execution of *Fall Gelb* was 12
November 1939, but – fortunately, in the eyes of many of
Hitler's generals – it had to be postponed because of bad
weather. It was, in fact, the first of fourteen such postpone-
ments between then and May 1940. In January, however, the
Wehrmacht was poised to strike, and D-Day was once again
fixed, this time for the 17th of that month. German forces
were moving up to their jump-off positions, and unit commanders were assembling at their respective headquarters for
final briefings.

So it was, on the morning of 10 January, that Major Hellmuth
Reinberger of the 22nd Airborne found himself in the cockpit
of the little Messerschmitt 108, on his way from Loddenheide
to Cologne with the operational orders for *Fall Gelb* tucked in
his briefcase.

Now, as the aircraft droned on, Reinberger began to feel
distinctly uneasy. The weather was beginning to deteriorate,
and he saw with apprehension that his pilot, Erich Hönmanns,
was peering anxiously over the side, trying to get his bear-
ings. Before long, with the visibility narrowing all the time,
Hönmanns realized that he was hopelessly lost and that without knowing it he had probably been driven across the Rhine,
miles off track, by a strong easterly wind. If that was so, the
Me 108 was now flying over enemy territory.

The pilot at once changed course, heading east in the hope
of sighting the river. A minute later the engines began to mis-
fire; the carburettor was icing up. Hönmanns juggled with the
engine controls, but it was no use. Soon the engine cut out

altogether, and he was left with no alternative but to make a forced landing.

Selecting a large, snow-covered field, he turned into wind and began his approach. At the last moment the pilot spotted a line of poplars in his path. It was too late to avoid them; all he could do was kick the rudder frantically and steer for what looked like a sizeable gap. A second later the aircraft shook violently as the trees ripped off both its wingtips; then it was down, lurching over the snow and coming to rest just short of the far hedge.

The two men scrambled from the cockpit with no worse injury than a severe shaking. After consulting their map, they decided that they had landed near Mechelen, just north of Maastricht, in Belgian territory. Reinberger immediately took shelter behind the hedge and set about trying to burn the precious documents. His lighter failed to work, and he had almost given up in despair when a Belgian peasant came up and obligingly offered him a match, with the aid of which he soon had a small fire going.

He was feeding the papers into it, sheet by sheet, when he heard shouts. Coming towards the crippled aircraft across the field were some Belgian soldiers. Hönmanns, hoping to buy enough time to enable Reinberger to finish his task, went to meet them halfway with his hands up in an attempt to convince them that he had been alone in the aircraft. However, a keen-eyed Belgian soon spotted the ribbon of smoke rising from behind the hedge, and a minute later Reinberger had been captured too – together with the documents, most of which were still intact.

The two men were taken to a nearby police post, where they were interrogated by a Belgian intelligence officer. During the proceedings, Reinberger saw that the documents were lying on a table nearby; he seized them and tried to thrust them into a stove, but they were rescued – charred but still legible – by the Belgian officer.

The documents were quickly passed on to the Dutch and French Governments. The latter at once placed its armies in a

B*

state of alert, and Billotte's Army Group One, moving through fearful conditions of snow and ice, closed up to the Belgian frontier, having been advised by the Belgian High Command that the necessary authority would be given for Allied forces to enter Belgian territory. This order, however, was immediately countermanded to King Leopold, who dismissed his Chief of Staff, and the French had no alternative but to pull back once more.

Meanwhile, Hitler had been informed of the incident on the morning of 11 January. He at once flew into one of his characteristic rages, threatening the death sentence for both Hönmanns and Reinberger and dismissing General Felmy, commanding Luftlotte 2, and replacing him with General Kesselring. Within forty-eight hours reports were reaching the German High Command of Belgian and Dutch mobilization, together with large-scale movements by the French Army. That same day, with the weather once again deteriorating, Hitler gave orders for the indefinite postponement of *Fall Gelb*; he also instructed his generals to re-shape the entire plan.

The generals received the decision with open relief; now, at last, they would have time to carry out the tactical manoeuvres that were badly needed if the Wehrmacht was to iron out the deficiencies that had been revealed in the Polish campaign. For the next month, the army training-areas at Mayen near Koblenz echoed to the rattle of tracks and the roar of engines as the Panzer divisions put their men and equipment through their paces.

During the course of the manoeuvres, several members of the General Staff – including Halder, the original architect of *Fall Gelb* – gradually came round to von Manstein's point of view that Sedan, and not Belgium, should be the '*Schwerpunkt*' or focal point of the offensive in the west. Hitler himself – who had not been apprised of Manstein's theories until now – expressed a keen interest in the idea, and on 17 February he summoned Manstein and several other supporters of the plan to a conference in Berlin. The following day, the plan was outlined to Brauchitsch and Halder, who were instructed to get together to work out all the necessary operational details.

The new draft of the invasion plan was ready by 24 February. It bore little resemblance to the original concept; the brunt of the assault would now be borne by Army Group A, with Army Group B acting in a diversionary capacity to draw the French into Holland and northern Belgium. The order of battle for the revised offensive, code-named '*Sichelschnitt*' ('Sickle Cut') would now be as follows. First, on the invasion's northernmost flank – opposite Holland and northern Belgium – would come von Bock's Army Group B, comprising Küchler's Eighteenth Army and Reichenau's Sixth Army; then Rundstedt's Army Group A, facing the Ardennes and the Meuse southwards from Liège and consisting of Kluge's Fourth Army, List's Twelfth Army and Busch's Sixteenth Army; and finally Army Group C under von Leeb, extending from Luxembourg to the Swiss frontier and made up of the First and Seventh Armies.

The three armies allotted to Rundstedt's Army Group A gave him a total of forty-five divisions. Only ten, however, would form the tip of the spear; those assigned to General Ewald von Kleist's Panzergruppe. This consisted of General Reinhardt's XLI Panzer Corps (6th and 8th Divisions), General Guderian's XIX Panzer Corps (1st, 2nd and 10th Divisions) and General von Wietersheim's XIV Motorized Corps of five divisions. Together, the two Panzer Corps totalled 1,264 tanks, added to which were the armoured vehicles of General Hoth's XV Panzer Corps (5th and 7th Divisions), which was to protect the Army Group's right flank. XV Corps was to cross the Meuse at Dinant and break through towards Brussels. The panzers would strike on a forty-five-mile-wide front, with Guderian's XIX Corps – supported by the elite Grossdeutschland Regiment of the SS and backed up by XIV Corps – concentrating on the '*Schwerpunkt*' of the battle at Sedan while Reinhardt's XLI Corps broke through at Monthermé.

As a diversionary measure, the nineteen infantry divisions of von Leeb's Army Group C were to launch a limited offensive against the Maginot Line to the south. In fact, this Army

Group was not destined to play a key part in the coming offensive; it was tied down to the secondary role of preventing the French from transferring troops from its sector to where the real battle would be fought in the north-east.

Although the *Sichelschnitt* plan was audacious enough, its architects were conscious that it was in the nature of a gamble, and a dangerous one at that. It depended wholly on the surprise rapier thrust of the German armour, supported by the Luftwaffe, and the very execution of the plan meant subjecting seventy-five per cent of the Wehrmacht's first-line divisions in the west to the risk of destruction should the French rally sufficiently to nip the armoured thrust in the flank as it debouched from the Ardennes. Moreover, there seemed to be no real plan for further exploitation once the initial breakthrough across the Meuse had been made. Decisions in this respect were to be left in the main to individual Corps commanders, as General Guderian found when he attended a staff conference in March:

Each of us generals outlined what his task was and how he intended to carry it out. I was the last to speak. My task was as follows: on the day ordered, I would cross the Luxembourg frontier, drive through southern Belgium towards Sedan, cross the Meuse and establish a bridgehead on the far side so that the infantry corps following behind could get across. I explained briefly that my corps would advance through Luxembourg and southern Belgium in three columns; I reckoned on reaching the Belgian frontier posts on the first day, and I hoped to break through them on that same day; on the second day I would advance as far as Neufchâteau; on the third day I would reach Bouillon and cross the Semois; on the fourth day I would arrive at the Meuse; on the fifth day I would cross it. By the evening of the fifth day I hoped to have established a bridgehead on the far bank. Hitler asked: 'And then what are you going to do?' He was the first person who had thought to ask me this vital question. I replied: 'Unless I receive orders to the contrary, I intend on the next day to continue my advance westwards. The supreme leadership must decide whether my objective is to be Amiens or Paris. In my opinion the correct course is to drive past Amiens to the English Channel.' Hitler

nodded and said nothing more. Only General Busch, who commanded the Sixteenth Army on my left, cried out: 'Well, I don't
think you'll cross the river in the first place!' Hitler, the tension
visible in his face, looked at me to see what I would reply. I said:
'There's no need for you to do so, in any case.' Hitler made no
comment.

I never received any further orders as to what I was to do once
the bridgehead over the Meuse was captured. All my decisions,
until I reached the Atlantic seaboard at Abbeville, were taken by
me and me alone. The Supreme Command's influence on my
actions was merely restrictive throughout.

Then there was the question of the quality of the German
armour itself. Although the ten Panzer divisions had a total
strength of some 2,700 tanks, only six hundred or so of these
were the modern Mark IIIs and IVs; the backbone of the divisions was still the Mark II, which was armed with a 20-mm
cannon and which was deficient in both armour and firepower.
There were also a considerable number of the old Mark Is of
1934 vintage – the Wehrmacht's first operational tank, armed
only with machine-guns – and four hundred Czech T.38 AFVs,
built by the Skoda factory and armed with a 37-mm gun. It
seemed a motley collection with which to undertake a major
drive deep into enemy territory, even though on Hitler's
orders most of the Mark IIIs and IVs belonging to von Bock's
Army Group B were transferred to Army Group A to strengthen
the latter's offensive capability.

Compared with the armour at the disposal of the Allies in
the spring of 1940, the Germans were actually numerically
inferior. Together, the French and British forces in north-
eastern France possessed just over three thousand armoured
fighting vehicles, and in quality too some of the Allied types
were superior. The Matilda tanks of the British Army Tank
Brigade, for example, were more heavily armoured than any
the Germans possessed, and although they were slower, their
2-pounder guns were more effective than the German 37-mm.
The French B Tank, too, was probably the best AFV in service
with any of the belligerents in 1940, despite its shortcomings,

and the splendid Somua cavalry tank could outshoot anything else in the field with its 47-mm high velocity gun. The French had a total of eight hundred B Tanks and Somuas in service by April 1940 – more than the number of German Marks III and IV.

Germany, however, held one major trump card: the Luftwaffe. It had suffered heavily during the Polish Campaign, having lost a total of 897 bombers and dive-bombers, 210 fighters and 474 reconnaissance and transport aircraft; but now, in March 1940, its combat squadrons were once more up to strength with a total of more than five thousand aircraft at their disposal. Some four thousand of these were on the inventories of Luftflotten (Air Fleets) 2 and 3, which were to provide the necessary air support for the invasion. In the north, Kesselring's Luftflotte 2 – comprising IV Fliegerkorps under General Alfred Keller and VIII Fliegerkorps commanded by General Wolfram von Richthofen (a cousin of the famous First World War ace) – was assigned to support Army Group B, while General Sperrle's Luftflotte 3, with Fliegerkorps I, II and V, was to operate in conjunction with Army Group A and part of Army Group C. Potentially the most dangerous to the Allies was von Richthofen's VIII Fliegerkorps, with its three wings of Junkers Ju 87 Stukas; they would be principally responsible for blasting a path ahead of the armour. To provide top cover for the bombers and dive-bombers, there were seven fighter wings, equipped with single-engined Messerschmitt 109 or twin-engined Messerschmitt 110 fighters.

Against this formidable line-up the French Armée de l'Air could muster only about twelve hundred combat aircraft for operations in the north-east, many of them obsolete. Bomber units were for the most part equipped with old Amiots and Blochs, and comparatively few of the new LeO 451s had been delivered; in the ground-attack field the first units were only just beginning to receive the excellent Breguet 693; and the fighter squadrons were equipped with a mixture of Morane 406s, Bloch 151s and American-built Curtiss Hawk 75s, with the first examples of the promising new Dewoitine D.520 in the process of being delivered. In short, the French aircraft industry was beginning to produce some superlative new equipment – too late.

In addition, the Royal Air Force had about six hundred aircraft in France, divided between Bomber Command's Advanced Air Striking Force and the BEF's Air Component. Mainstay of the former were the eight squadrons of outdated Fairey Battle light bombers, with two squadrons of the more modern Bristol Blenheims, supported by two squadrons of Hurricanes; the Air Component of the BEF had four squadrons of Blenheims, two of Hurricanes, two of Gloster Gladiator biplane fighters and five of Westland Lysander army co-operation aircraft. Several more Blenheim squadrons were standing by in England to be transferred to France if the Germans attacked; in the event, they never arrived.

The opposing air forces had been skirmishing with one another right from the outbreak of hostilities, clashing over the frontiers, and losses on both sides had not been light. In December 1939, the AASF's Battles had been withdrawn from daylight operations after receiving a severe mauling at the hands of the Messerschmitts over the Saar, and the lightly-armed French reconnaissance aircraft, probing into enemy territory day after day, were shot to ribbons or staggered back to their bases with smoking engines and their crews dead or dying. As a result of these losses, all reconnaissance units were restricted to night operations from October 1939, a fact that was to prove a severe handicap for Allied intelligence.

Between 3 September 1939 and 1 May 1940, the French Air Force lost 914 aircraft of all types – many of them acciden-tally. The Luftwaffe's losses over the same period were 937 combat aircraft destroyed or badly damaged from all causes, in addition to the losses sustained in the Polish campaign. For the aircrews on both sides, the expression 'Phoney War' had little meaning; the first phase of the Battle for France was fought here, high above the Franco-German border, and young men paid with their lives for the vital prize of air supremacy.

On the ground, it was a different story. It was hard to believe that there was a war on at all. With the coming of spring,

French troops in the front line played games, tended gardens and even raised animals in miniature farms behind their positions – while their defences were neglected. Even training went by the board, and what there was in the way of manœuvres was so poorly organized as to be worthless. For the British troops in France, too, life was rather like an organized holiday punctuated by one or two annoying spells of training and digging defences. One former BEF soldier, Ken Carter, recalls:

I was with the 150th Infantry Brigade of the 50th Northumbrian Division. We landed at Cherbourg in early January and from there we travelled through a bitterly cold French winter to Le Mans to complete our training before being moved up to the Belgian border to take up our war station. After some weeks in the freezing cold at Le Mans, the Brigade, which consisted of the 4th and 5th Battalions of the Green Howards and the 4th Battalion of the East Yorkshires – all Territorial units – moved up through Arras, Amiens and Lille before settling down for a period in Wavrin and the surrounding villages about twenty miles from Lille. There we carried out exercises with regular units of the British and French armies and also built fortifications and tank traps in the path of a likely German attack through Holland and Belgium.

In spite of continuous exercises and one of the coldest winters in living memory, life was not at all bad as far as the troops were concerned. This was virtually peacetime France; there was no rationing of any kind, with the exception of petrol, prices in the shops and cafés were very reasonable, and entertainment by leading English stars of the day was laid on in theatres wherever British troops were stationed. Nevertheless, although there was a general air of optimism, many of us felt that it couldn't last. There had to be a nasty surprise around the corner somewhere.

The 'nasty surprise' was not long in coming. On 9 April 1940 the Germans struck – not on the Western Front but in Norway. In the ten days that followed, a hastily-assembled Anglo-French Expeditionary Force landed at Narvik, Namsos and Andalsnes, but after two weeks of bitter fighting the Allies had lost every foothold except Narvik itself. The battle was by no means over, but by the beginning of May the situation of the German forces in Norway had improved to such an extent that the German High Command could once again focus its attention on the west. For the Allies, the long months of un-reality were over.

Soon after midnight on 10 May 1940, the pilot of a French aircraft carrying out a reconnaissance between the French border and Düsseldorf sighted long convoys of vehicles, head-lights full on, streaming westwards over the German roads of the Rhineland. On returning to base, he immediately tried to raise his duty officer on the telephone, anxious to pass on the news to higher authority. But the duty officer had left orders not to be disturbed. It was half an hour before the pilot suc-ceeded in getting him out of bed and rousing him sufficiently to make a report.

Finally, with a sigh of relief, he finished talking and hung up. As he walked towards his billet, together with his observer, he paused; from the east there came the rumble of what sounded like thunder. He shrugged and went on his way, the warm breeze of the May night on his face. Dawn would soon be breaking. It was exactly 03.30 hours.

CHAPTER 2

Belgium and Holland, 10 - 15 May

Belgium

The defenders of the Belgian fortress of Eben Emael, the men of the 7th Infantry Regiment, had been on full alert now since 02.00 hours, peering apprehensively into the darkness that lay heavily over the fourteen-mile strip of Dutch territory that lay like a barrier between Belgian and German soil at this point. Almost every man sensed instinctively that the storm from the east was about to break, and yet there was also a feeling that it would sweep past and leave Eben Emael unscathed. The men of the 7th Infantry, after all, knew that even the strongest assault would batter itself fruitlessly to extinction against the fortress, which was the most impregnable structure of its kind in the world. Sited on a plateau on the west bank of the Albert Canal, the fort measured a thousand yards long by two hundred yards wide at its broadest part. On its north-eastern flank it ended in a sheer 150 foot drop into the canal. Its other flanks were protected by wide anti-tank ditches which in turn were covered by blockhouses mounting searchlights, heavy machine-guns and 2-inch anti-tank weapons. Inside the perimeter, heavily reinforced concrete and metal bunkers covered every inch of the ground with their field of fire. Any troops who managed to get across the ditches would at once be caught in the deadly crossfire of dozens of weapons with calibres ranging from the .5-inch of the machine-guns to the 3-inch muzzles of the artillery.

There was no doubt that the architects of Eben Emael had known their job. It was even more invulnerable than Fort Douaumont at Verdun, which had held out for so long against the full weight of German artillery and troops in 1916. As the key to the Albert Canal defences and guardian of the gateway to Liège, as the wall which was designed to withstand the blows of the German battering-ram for at least five days until the French Army and British Expeditionary Force could be fully committed to the conflict under the terms of the Allied Dyle Plan, Eben Emael was unsurpassed – by 1916 standards. But this was 1940, and in the plans for the defence of Eben Emael there was one serious omission. No one had thought to provide the fortress with anti-aircraft weapons, nor, indeed, had the possibility of an airborne assault been seriously countenanced.

Now, at 04.00 on this morning of 10 May, the German battering-ram which was to shatter the fortress of Eben Emael from a new and totally unexpected direction was already within minutes of striking. Thirty minutes earlier, forty-one Junkers 52 transports of I and II KGR ZBV (*Kampfgruppe zum Besonderen Verwendung* – Special Duties Wing) 172 had taken off from the airfields of Butzweilerhof and Ostheim on opposite banks of the Rhine near Cologne and set course westwards in a long stream, guided by a line of flashing navigational beacons stretching all the way to Aachen. Beyond the beacons, along the frontiers of Belgium and Holland, the massed divisions of Wehrmacht were poised ready to hurl themselves like a steel flood into the Low Countries.

Behind each JU 52, at the end of its towrope, swayed a DFS 230 heavy assault glider, laden with troops and equipment. For six months the glider assault troops – all of them sappers who had volunteered for airborne training – had been preparing for this mission under conditions of strict secrecy at a training-school at Hildesheim. Known as Assault Group Koch after its commander, Captain Koch, the unit had been subjected to strict security precautions during its long period of training. The men had been allowed no leave and had been forbidden to mix with men of other units. Their mail had been strictly censored and each soldier had been required to sign the following declaration: ' I am aware that I shall risk sentence of death should I, by intent or carelessness, make known to another person by spoken word, text or illustration, anything concerning the base at which I am serving.'

In fact, secrecy was so stringent that although each man knew the details of the part the others had to play in the operation, they were to learn each other's names only after the operation was over. After lengthy classroom sessions, the men had undergone training by day and night and in every kind of weather, and in December 1939 the finalized operation was rehearsed against the former Czech fortifications in the Altvatar district of the Sudetenland. First Lieutenant Rudolf Witzig, one of the officers in the operation, later commented: 'We developed a healthy respect for what lay ahead of us. After a while our confidence reached the stage where we, the attackers, believed our position outside of the breastworks safer than that of the defenders inside.'

It was only during the briefing in the hours before the take-off that the men of Assault Group Koch had learned the true identity of their objective. The forty-one gliders were in fact divided into four waves, each with a specific objective. The task of capturing Eben Emael was assigned to Assault Detachment Granite, which consisted of eleven gliders carrying eighty-five men under Witzig's command. The second Assault Detachment, Concrete, with ninety-six men in eleven gliders, was to capture the bridge over the Maas at Vroenhoven and prevent its destruction by the defenders. The third Assault Detachment, Steel, had as its objective the bridge at Veldwezelt over the Albert Canal to the north of Vroenhoven. Steel consisted of nine gliders carrying ninety-two men. The third bridge over the canal, at Kanne, was the target of ten gliders and ninety soldiers of Assault Detachment Iron.

Although take-off and assembly had been faultless, trouble hit the formation, or rather the leading echelon consisting of Assault Detachment Granite, minutes after the armada set course. The pilot of the eleventh and last Junkers in this wave, seeing what appeared to be the blue exhaust flames of another aircraft suddenly loom up ahead of him, took violent evasive action. The Army glider pilot desperately tried to follow suit but he was not quick enough. The towrope parted under the strain, and the glider dropped away, turning back across the Rhine to land in a meadow near Cologne. It was particularly unfortunate that this glider carried First Lieutenant Witzig, the commander of Assault Detachment Granite. While his men worked to turn the field into an emergency landing-strip, he unpacked his collapsible bicycle and pedalled down the road towards Ostheim, catching a lift from a passing motorist. He arrived at the airfield shortly after four o'clock and explained the situation to the duty officer, who at once contacted Gutersloh to arrange for a replacement aircraft. The second mishap of the night involved the pilot of another glider in Assault Detachment Granite, who thought he saw his towing aircraft flash the signal to cast off. He pulled the towrope release, and the glider landed in a field near Düren, not half way to the frontier. Its occupants had no alternative but to commandeer some transport and make their way to where the Wehrmacht units were poised for the main thrust into the Low Countries.

The rest of the force flew on. Because of the rigid radio silence the other members of Assault Detachment Granite were not aware that their numbers had been seriously depleted. Ahead of them now in the distance a lone searchlight probed upwards. It was a marker, and at its base lay Aachen. The Junkers had been climbing steadily all the way, and by the time they reached that last beacon their altitude would be eight thousand feet. Another fifteen minutes and they would be over the junction of the Dutch, German and Belgian borders. Then the Junkers would turn away, and the gliders would sweep silently down towards their objectives.

At 04.15 the Junkers of Assault Detachment Granite released their gliders, now reduced to nine in number, and turned away towards Maastricht where they had the task of dropping dummies festooned with fire-crackers to confuse the Belgian defences. As they did so, sporadic anti-aircraft fire came up, and the garrison at Eben Emael, seeing the flurry of anti-aircraft fire shells flicker across the sky, believed that this was the signal that German bombers were crossing the frontier and strained their ears to catch the sound of engines. They heard nothing and relaxed a little. Seconds later a black shadow swept in low from the east and slid across the ground between two blockhouses, coming to a halt on a clear patch a hundred yards from a machine-gun bunker. The dazed Belgian gunners strove frantically to depress and traverse the barrels of their weapons as more gliders touched down.

Soldiers burst from the first glider and fanned out towards their objective, bunker no. 19. The machine-gun stammered, firing blindly. A German NCO crouched by the bunker wall and dropped a satchel of high explosive through the periscope slit in the armoured dome. There was the dull thud of an explosion, and the chatter of the machine-gun stopped abruptly. Then came a sudden burst of gunfire in the southern corner of the fort; tracers lanced out into the half light, and three German soldiers fell. The rest went into action and laid an explosive charge against the wall of the bunker. A moment later the stunned defenders staggered out into the open through the shattered cupola, their hands on their heads.

Within ten minutes as many bunkers had been destroyed. However, by this time the Belgians had realized that the attacking force consisted of only seventy-odd men. The garrison commander rang the CO of a nearby artillery battery and asked him to lay a barrage on the fort itself. Soon, the earth was erupting among the abandoned gliders, and the attackers themselves were forced to seek cover in the shattered bunkers. Reeling under the barrage of artillery fire, the Germans prepared to fight it out, holding on if possible until the main Wehrmacht thrust reached the canal. For three hours a pitched battle raged under the drifting smoke that obscured Eben Emael; then at 07.30 the unexpected happened. A glider winged in through the smoke and rumbled to a stop near the range of bunker no. 19. It was First Lieutenant Witzig and his men, who had at last reached the battle after being pulled out of the meadow near Cologne by the Junkers from Gutersloh. Witzig took

command from Sergeant Wenzel, who had directed operations
so far.

A few minutes later, a flight of Heinkel 111s roared overhead and dropped several containers of badly-needed ammunition to the German sappers, who renewed their attack on
the remaining bunkers. Hour after hour the battle swayed
backwards and forwards, the Belgians fighting stubbornly for
every square foot of ground. At last Witzig managed to establish radio contact with Storm Groups Concrete and Iron at
Vroenhoven and Kanne. The news he received was not good.
It appeared that the bridges in Maastricht itself had been destroyed by the defenders, and the one at Kanne, which linked
Maastricht with Eben Emael, had been blown up just as the
assault gliders touched down. However, the main bridges at
Vroenhoven and Veldwezelt had been captured intact, although
they had subsequently come under heavy Belgian fire. Across
these two bridges the Panzer divisions were pouring into the
Low Countries.

All that day and all the next night Storm Group Granite
clung desperately to its foothold in Eben Emael. The Germans
received excellent air support throughout from the Henschel
123s of 11/LG2 and the Junkers 87s of StG2, which carried out
very precise dive bombing attacks. Finally, at 07.00 on 11
May, the weary, unshaven soldiers were relieved by shock
troops who proceeded to wipe out all remaining resistance.
By noon it was all over. In the clear sunshine under a sky
dappled with cirrus cloud, the twelve hundred surviving defenders, dazed and bewildered, threw down their weapons and
marched into captivity under the sub-machine-guns of the
victors. Eben Emael had fallen, and the way was now open for
the armoured spearheads of von Bock's Army Group B, spreading out across the drab Belgian plain west of the Meuse.

The early hours of that disastrous 10 May were characterized by a second noteworthy airborne operation. Before dawn,
as the gliders were about to go down on Eben Emael, twenty-
five Fieseler Storch Army Co-operation aircraft, renowned for
their short take-off and landing performance, had deposited

125 volunteers of the 34th Infantry Division near Esch-sur-Alzette on the Franco-Luxembourg border. The task of the detachment, commanded by Lieutenant Hedderich, was to hold the crossroads at Esch until General Heinz Guderian's Panzers arrived. The Storchs made two sorties, and by first light the task force was in position. One of their first contacts was a bewildered *gendarme*, who politely informed them that they were on neutral territory and asked them to leave. Equally as politely, the Germans arrested him. There were no further incidents before the German ground forces arrived. By 09.00 the forward elements of the 1st Panzer Division had reached the Belgian frontier after rumbling across the whole of Luxembourg with hardly a shot fired.

The second airborne operation ran along similar lines and took place further north, in the Belgian Ardennes. Here, two assault groups, composed of the 3rd Battalion of the elite Grossdeutschland Regiment and the special volunteer force, some four hundred men in all, were to be landed at Nives and Witry, about halfway between Neufchâteau and the frontier towns of Bastogne and Martelange. Neufchâteau, situated on the heights with roads radiating from it in all directions, was a vital defensive position, and its capture was essential to Guderian's rapid advance on Sedan. The operation, code-named 'Niwi' began at 04.20 on 10 May when ninety-eight Storchs carrying 196 troops took off from Bitburg and Deckendorf and headed for their objectives. Everything did not go entirely as planned. Although the first formation of fifty-six Storchs landed their troops at Witry on schedule, the Nives group of forty-two aircraft became badly scattered, and some of the Storchs landed as much as nine miles from their objective. It was not until the afternoon that the two assault groups were able to link up, by which time the Storchs had flown in the second half of the force. Witry was secured at 13.00 after a stiff fight between the Germans and troops of the 1st Regiment Ardennais, which was joined by the vanguard of the French 5th Machine-Gun Regiment. Sporadic fighting continued until the early evening, when the Franco-Belgian force withdrew upon the arrival of the leading tanks of the 1st Panzers. The road to Neufchâteau was open.

Meanwhile, the Luftwaffe was operating at maximum effort. Between dawn and dusk on 10 May, formations of German bombers varying in strength from three to thirty machines attacked seventy-two allied air bases in Holland, Belgium and France. Forty-seven of these airfields were in northern, eastern and central France, but they were bombed by only small groups of aircraft, the Luftwaffe's main effort being concentrated on Holland, and the damage they inflicted was surprisingly light. Other raids were broken up by French and British fighters which scored a number of victories in the course of the day. There were also inevitable mistakes on the Luftwaffe's part. In the early afternoon, for example, three Heinkel 111s detailed to attack Dijon bombed the German town of Freiburg-im-Breisgau by mistake, killing fifty-seven civilians. Part of the trouble was that the Luftwaffe crews had been given no prior warning of the offensive; they had been woken up in the early hours and ordered to attend a briefing at fifteen minutes' notice, and flight planning by individual crews was consequently not as thorough as it might have been.

Nevertheless, during that first day of the invasion, the Luftwaffe carried out some seventy-five air attacks on Belgian airfields, destroying thirty machines on the ground. Total Belgian losses in the air and on the ground by midday on the 10th were fifty-three machines, almost one third of the Belgian Air Force's total first-line strength. This attrition, coupled with the loss of the fortress at Eben Emael and the bridges at Maastricht, threw the whole Belgian defensive plan into jeopardy. By noon on the 10th the armoured echelons of General Hoeppner's XVI Corps, the 3rd and 4th Panzer Divisions, were across the Maastricht bridges and hurling themselves on the 7th Belgian division holding the centre of the Belgian line. By early afternoon the 4th Panzer had reached Tongeren, breaking up some Belgian cavalry units and putting them to flight. At 18.00 hours the tanks reached Waremme.

Meanwhile, the two divisions of the French Cavalry Corps,

the 2nd Light Armoured Division and the 3rd, which had assembled south of the Forêt de Mormal, had begun to move up to the assistance of the Belgians in the early morning of the 10th. By late afternoon the leading armoured car squadrons of the 12th Cuirassiers had bypassed the Petite-Gette and were approaching Hasselt and Tongeren, while to the south of Liège the 8th Cuirassiers were on the River Ourthe between Comblain-au-Pont and Durbuy, their right flank in contact with the advance parties of the 4th Cavalry Division of the French Ninth Army. During the night of the 10th/11th, the 12th Cuirassiers skirmished with German patrols near Tongeren, while the 8th, together with reconnaissance groups of v Corps and the 5th North African Division occupied the line of the Mehaigne down to Huy and the Meuse through Ardenne to Namur. By daybreak, the bulk of the French Cavalry Corps, pushing forward through the retreating Belgian Cavalry, had occupied positions on the Petite-Gette and the Tirlemont-Huy road. The Belgian Cavalry Corps was now trying to regroup between Tirlemont and Halen, while the badly battered Belgian 14th Division had fallen back on Lummen.

General Prioux, commanding the French Cavalry Corps, whose troops had reached the Dyle Line after advancing up to ninety-five miles during the course of the night, was horrified to discover that no proper Belgian defences existed – contrary to his information. Moreover the Belgians were retreating as fast as they could, and confusion reigned everywhere. Prioux, realizing it would be impossible to hold the French positions when the Germans attacked in strength, in view of the collapse of the Belgians, strongly advocated abandoning the Dyle positions in favour of the Escaut defensive plan. It was clear that the French Cavalry would be unable to defend the line against the German armoured push for long enough to allow the First Army to establish itself.

General Billotte, however, was of the opinion that with the leading elements of the French and British forces already on the Dyle Line and the main bodies of allied troops moving up towards the front, a change of plan at this stage would be

disastrous. Nevertheless, he relu
French Cavalry Corps was in sei
draw to a line on the Ardenne-Pe
meantime, everything was to be
ment of the French First Army a
Force on the Dyle-Gembloux line.

For General Prioux's Cavalry C
grim. The Corps was about to be
assault as part of the German XVI
the Gembloux Gap; the retreat

Dyle Line left Prioux's two divisions, their combined strength
only two-thirds that of one Panzer division, as the sole obstacle
in the path of the next advance by the Panzers that had
breached the Albert Canal-Meuse positions. The French troops
dug in along the twenty-four miles of the Tirlemont-Wavre
line and awaited the assault that was to come.

Meanwhile, reconnaissance groups of the III, IV and V Corps
were speeding forward to strengthen the Cavalry Corps. The
main body of the infantry began its march towards the front
on the morning of 11 May. Only one division in each Corps
was motorized; the 1st in III Corps, the 15th in IV and the
12th in V. The other three divisions, the 2nd North African,
the Moroccan and the 5th North African, were all normal
active divisions designed to move rapidly on foot. The lightning advance of the Germans, however, made nonsense of the
conventional French Army plans for the movement of large
bodies of troops. What was needed was transport, and a lot of
it. Divisions scraped together what transport they could, but
even then the majority of the troops still had to proceed on
foot. They were ordered to double their length of march in
the course of the day, and by the time they reached their
advance positions, most of them were already exhausted. The
whole project for manning the Dyle position collapsed in confusion. Of III Corps, the 1st Division was in position on the
13th but of the 2nd North African, only the infantry had
arrived. Of IV Corps, General Juin's 15th Motorized arrived
early and was able to lay a minefield ahead of its positions,

as only partly completed. The advance of v
General René Altmayer also proceeded slowly,
complicated by the fact that the destination of
forward battalion was north-east of Namur, where it
mixed with the 2nd Chasseurs Ardennais. It was the
orning of the 15th before its rear units reached the front,
after marching for three days.

The Belgian Air Force meanwhile continued to fight valiantly with its surviving obsolescent equipment. The most
numerous type was the Fairey Fox biplane, which equipped
the majority of reconnaissance and bomber reconnaissance
units as well as one fighter escadrille of the 2nd Regiment.
They were supplemented by 13 Fairey Battles of the 3rd Regiment, together with a handful of Gloster Gladiators and Fiat
CR42s. It was the antiquated Foxes of the 2nd Regiment that
were the first to encounter the Messerschmitts in combat over
Belgium. At 08.35 on 10 May, nine Foxes took off from
Brustheim to intercept a formation of enemy bombers when
they were bounced by about fifteen Messerschmitt 109ES. Two
of the Foxes were quickly shot down. The remainder, their
fabric shot to ribbons and with some of their pilots wounded,
managed to escape. By 12 May the Belgian Air Force had virtually ceased to exist; its bases were graveyards of wrecked aircraft caught on the ground between sorties. The Gladiators of
the 1st Escadrille managed to fly a few sorties before they
were knocked out, but on the morning of 14 May the entire
Belgian fighter force consisted of six Fiat CR42s operating from
a small emergency landing ground eight miles west of Antwerp.
At 11.45 that morning, the Fiats took off to provide cover for
the French troops embarking at the Fleurus railway station
near Charleroi. It was destined to be their last mission over
Belgian territory before evacuating to new locations in northern France.

Elsewhere, the allied air forces were being massacred by the
hordes of prowling Messerschmitts.

After a lengthy delay, French GHQ had at last given the go-
ahead to Air Marshal Barratt, commanding the British Air

Forces in France, and General d'Astier de la Vigerie, commanding the Northern Zone of air operations, to unleash their bombers against the flood of men and material pouring through the Ardennes and over the river at Maastricht. The first attacks, against enemy columns advancing through Luxembourg, were carried out in the afternoon of 10 May by the Battle squadrons of the Advanced Air Striking Force; twenty-three aircraft out of sixty-four failed to return, the victims of the flak and Messerschmitts, and as many more were so badly damaged as to be out of action for some time. So bad was the rate of attrition, in fact, that the AASF was able to carry out only one attack on the 11th. Eight Battles set out; only one came back. On this day one of the AASF's Blenheim squadrons, No. 114, was almost completely wiped out on the ground when German bombers attacked its base at Vraux.

In the evening of the 11th, the French bomber force carried out its first mission of the war when five LeO 451s attacked enemy columns in the Maastricht-Tongeren area. One LeO was shot down and all the rest severely damaged. That night Blenheims of RAF Bomber Command, operating from Britain, attacked the bridges at Maastricht, but they caused no damage. Four aircraft failed to return.

The AASF's other Blenheim squadron, No. 139, took off at first light on 12 May to attack an enemy column near Tongeren. They never reached the target. They were caught by the Messerschmitts and massacred; only two of the nine bombers returned to base. A few hours later, five Fairey Battles of No. 12 Squadron launched a heroic and suicidal attack on the Maastricht bridges, diving through an umbrella of 120 Messerschmitts and murderous flak. All the Battles were shot down. The leader of the attack, Flying Officer Garland, and his observer, Flight Sergeant Gray, were posthumously awarded the Victoria Cross.

The slaughter went on as the AASF hurled its dwindling resources against the bridgeheads. During the day's operations, sixty-two per cent of the Battles sent out failed to return, as did forty per cent of No. 2 Group's UK-based Blenheims. The

French also suffered heavily; in one attack on the bridges, they lost eight out of twelve Breguet 693 bombers. Yet the worst was still to come.

Meanwhile, by noon on 11 May, the Belgian forts around Liège had been completely surrounded, and although their garrisons continued to fight for several more days, their position was hopeless. Fort Pepinster capitulated only after the armistice with Belgium; its garrison, having much impressed the Germans by their valour, were allowed to march out with their arms shouldered and colours flying. By noon on 11 May, Hoeppner's xvi Panzer Corps had advanced a considerable way into Belgium, pushing back the divisions of 11 Corps on the Albert Canal. On the 12th the Germans entered St Trond and pushed on towards Hannu, which was held by a battalion of the 11th Dismounted Dragoons and a squadron of the 2nd Cuirassiers. A simultaneous attack was launched on Thismes and Crehen, near the junction with the 2nd Light Armoured. The French held on to Crehen all through the day, and there was a good deal of desperate fighting. The Panzers tore the French Hotchkiss tanks with their ancient 37-mm guns to shreds. By nightfall the Dragoon battalion had been wiped out and of what remained of the Hotchkiss squadron, less than fifty per cent got away under cover of darkness.

Holland

At 05.00 hours on 10 May, twenty-eight Heinkel 111s of the Luftwaffe's Kampfgeschwader 4 took off from their bases at Fassberg, Gutersloh and Delmenhorst and set course northwards, crossing the German coast near Wilhelmshaven. Over the Frisian Islands they turned to port, following the line of the Dutch coast in a great arc as far as The Hague. They then turned inland, running in from the west towards their target, the airport of Waalhaven on the outskirts of Rotterdam.

The Heinkel's circuitous route was designed to confuse the Dutch defences, but it failed in this primary purpose. The

Dutch had been on the alert for several hours, and as the bombers thundered over the coast, they ran into a heavy flak barrage. To make matters worse, the early morning sun was in the pilots' eyes and they failed to see the Dutch fighters attacking from ahead in a shallow dive until the latter were right on top of the bomber formation. The Dutch aircraft, nimble little Fokker D21s, swept through the German formation like a whirlwind, and a Heinkel fell away, its wings a sheet of flame and the crew baling out in its wake. The fighters continued to harry the Heinkels as they sped on towards their target. Elsewhere in the Dutch sky, other fighters were attacking formations of German bombers which were bearing down on the airfields of Amsterdam – Schiphol, Ypenburg and Bergen-op-Zoom, in a massive onslaught designed to smash the Dutch air defences in one blow.

Despite the determined efforts of the Dutch fighters, the Heinkels of KG4 swept across Waalhaven and unloaded their bombs with great accuracy. One stick fell across the hangars which collapsed in an inferno of fire and smoke, killing more than two hundred troops of the Dutch Queen's Regiment who were billeted inside. Meanwhile a second formation of aircraft – coming from the east this time, out of the sunrise – droned steadily towards the pall of smoke that marked Waalhaven. They were the three-engined Junkers 52 transports of KGRZBVI and they carried the paratroops of the 3rd Battalion, 1st Fallschirmjager Regiment. As they maintained a steady six hundred feet on the approach to the target, the Junkers 52 pilots got a momentary glimpse of KG4's Heinkels as they flashed overhead on their way home. Seconds later the first sticks of parachutes were going down and in five minutes the sky over Waalhaven was studded with white canopies as the paratroops descended in a great ring around the airfield perimeter.

Despite the pounding they had received, the Dutch defences were still able to put up a considerable amount of anti-aircraft fire. One Junkers was hit and swerved violently off course, spilling its cargo of paratroops into the burning hangars. There were no survivors. The bulk of the paratroops landed on target and went into action as soon as they hit the ground, closing in on the Dutch defences. Amid the clatter of small arms fire, six more JU52s landed on the airfield, paratroops spilling from them as they rolled to a stop and fanning out to engage the Dutch defensive positions. Within thirty minutes Waalhaven was in German hands and the last pockets of resistance were being mopped up. The stunned Dutch troops, unable to comprehend the disaster that had overwhelmed them, were shepherded into one of the surviving hangars which had been turned into a makeshift POW cage.

The securing of Waalhaven heralded the arrival of more transports and by 08.00 the airfield was crammed with JU52s, using every available inch of space. Overhead, twin-engined Messerschmitt 110 fighters maintained a continual air umbrella. At 08.30 there was a sudden alarm as the Netherlands Army Aviation threw its depleted bomber arm into action in a vain attempt to stop the enemy flood tide. Somehow, three antiquated Fokker TV bombers of No. 1 Squadron, First Air Regiment, managed to evade the Messerschmitt patrols for long enough to drop a few bombs on the parked JU52s, a few of which were hit and set on fire. Then the Messerschmitts pounced. Two of the TVs were shot down in flames within seconds; the third managed to get away. Shortly afterwards, the Dutch First Air Regiment tried again, this time with five Fokker CX biplanes. Two of them were destroyed before they reached the target; the others made a single strafing pass over the transports on the ground and succeeded in getting away, all of them severely damaged.

At the airfields of Valkenburg and Ypenburg, where a total of fifty JU52s had landed, it was the same story. At noon three Fokker CXs and eight Fokker CVs of the 2nd Air Regiment made a suicidal attack on the two airfields. Five of the CVs were shot down by the prowling Messerschmitts. At 12.30, in desperation, the Dutch Government requested the intervention of the Royal Air Force, and at 14.00 six Blenheim IVFs of No. 600 Squadron, operating out of Manston in Kent, swept across the Dutch coast towards Waalhaven. All but one were shot down by the Messerschmitt 110s of Zerstorer-Geschwader 1. Later in the afternoon, a more successful attack was made on Waalhaven by the Blenheims of No. 15 Squadron, operating from Alconbury in Huntingdonshire. They succeeded in destroying several JU52s, and all the British aircraft returned to base, although some of them had suffered extensive damage. Simultaneously, twelve Blenheims of No. 40 Squadron from RAF Wyton attacked Ypenburg. Nine aircraft bombed the primary target; another bombed a small landing-ground five miles west of Leyden, and an eleventh machine strafed some Junkers 52s parked along the beach between The Hague and Noordwijk. Three Blenheims failed to return, two being shot down by anti-aircraft fire and the third by Messerschmitts.

Although the Luftwaffe enjoyed complete air superiority, the airborne invasion was encountering serious resistance all over Holland, and in some areas things were going badly wrong for the Germans. At Ypenburg, north of Delft, the first wave of Junkers 52s had been virtually wiped out, with eleven out of thirteen aircraft destroyed by flak and obstacles on the airfield itself. Small groups of survivors succeeded in extricating themselves from the wreckage only to be mown down by Dutch machine-guns. More Junkers 52s littered the beach north of the The Hague where they presented excellent targets for the Dutch airmen who, braving the Messerschmitt air-cover and flying ancient Fokker CSs, CVs and CXs, carried out strafing attacks on the dunes throughout the day, destroying considerable quantities of equipment and killing many paratroops. Dutch resistance in this area was so effective in fact that by nightfall the German forces in The Hague area had ceased to be combat effective.

It was not long before Lieutenant-General Graf Sponeck, the commander of the airborne forces, his men pinned down by heavy Dutch fire among the dunes behind the carcases of the Junkers 52s that littered the beaches, realized that his main objective – an assault on The Hague, the seat of the Dutch Government and the royal family – would be out of the ques-

c

tion. At 19.00 hours, with no sign of any improvement in the situation, he established radio contact with Field Marshal Kesselring, commanding Luftflotte 2, and requested further instructions. Kesselring ordered him to forget about the assault on The Hague and try to group his men for an attack on Rotterdam. Sponeck promised to do what he could but he was sceptical about his chances of success; it was all his men could do to maintain their tenuous foothold on the coast, let alone go over to the offensive.

Elsewhere, too, the German timetable for the speedy occupation of Holland, which was vital in order to make the invasion's northern flank secure, was badly disrupted. The main obstacles in the Germans' path were the Rivers Maas and Rhine, whose wide estuaries formed a great natural barrier over which there were only four major crossing-points: the bridges in the centre of Rotterdam, Moerdijk and Dordrecht to be captured by German airborne forces in a lightning attack, after which they were to be held until the 9th Panzer Division fought its way through to them. Once this was achieved, the way in the fortress of Holland would be wide open.

Before this could be attempted, however, the bridges at Maastricht had to be secured, opening the way for the flood of infantry and Panzers coming from the east. The task of capturing the Maastricht bridges was assigned to a sub-unit known as the Bau and Lehr-Kompanie Brandenburg (Construction and Training Company Brandenburg) a tough commando unit formed in October 1939 and operating under the direct control of German Military Intelligence. In the early hours of 10 May, a party of Brandenburgers led by a Lieutenant Hocke and dressed in Dutch uniforms, with sub-machine-guns under their greatcoats, marched up to the Maastricht bridge masquerading as a party of Dutch troops who had captured some infiltrating Germans. The Dutch defenders of the bridge, however, were wide awake, and opened up with small arms fire. In the ensuing exchange, several Brandenburgers, including Lieutenant Hocke, were killed; the remainder scattered and were pinned down with no hope of succeeding in their primary objective, which was to remove the explosive charges which the Dutch had positioned on the bridges. A short while later, the Dutch blew up both bridges at Maastricht, with the result that the advance units of the German Sixth Army became hopelessly bogged down on the east bank of the Maas. A similar attempt to capture a bridge at Arnhem also ended in failure, but a third party of Brandenburgers did succeed in capturing a secondary bridge over the Maas at Gennep, enabling the 9th Panzer to push on and interpose itself between the Dutch Army and General Giraud's Seventh Army. The bridge at Gennep was also used by advance units of General von Reichenau's Sixth Army while engineers worked hard to repair the damage to the bridges at Maastricht.

The bridges at Rotterdam, Moerdijk and Dordrecht, meanwhile, had been assigned to General Student's 7th Flieger Division. Early on 10 May, while JU87 Stukas attacked defensive positions on the banks of the Maas, 120 men of the 11th Company, 16th Infantry Regiment, jumped from JU52 transports and captured the Moerdijk and Dordrecht bridges intact. The Dutch counter-attacked furiously at Dordrecht but the paras managed to hold on. The bridge at Moerdijk was especially vital, for with its capture vanished all hope of assistance to the beleaguered Dutch from General Giraud's Seventh Army. To capture the bridges over the Maas in the centre of Rotterdam, the Germans had devised a daring scheme. At 07.00 on the 10th, as the German troops consolidated their positions at Waalhaven, twelve curious aircraft came roaring along the Nieuwe Maas, six coming from the east and six from the west, converging on Rotterdam. They were the Heinkel HE59 biplanes of KGRZVB18, a unit whose normal task was air/sea rescue. On this occasion, each HE59 carried no less than ten fully-equipped stormtroops. From their base at Bad Zwischenahn, the two flights of six floatplanes had followed separate courses so that they would approach Rotterdam from opposite directions. Under the noses of the startled Dutch forces, the Heinkels touched down on the water and taxied towards the big Willems Bridge; the troops scrambled into rubber dinghies and paddled frantically for the river banks. Within minutes they were crouching behind girders of the twin bridges, heavy machine-guns in position.

As the HE59s roared away, their job done, the Dutch launched their first counter-attack. Bullets whined among the girders and chipped splinters of concrete from the bridge walls. The Germans kept up a brisk fire, and the Dutchmen fell back, unable to get a foothold on either bridge. A few minutes later a tram came rumbling up to the bridges from the south; from it leaped a company of German paratroops, fifty strong. They had been dropped a short distance south of the Maas to assist in the capture of the bridges. Dropping under cover beside their comrades, the new arrivals set up their machine-guns, surrounded themselves with belts and clips of ammunition and prepared for a bitter fight. Even so, they could not know that the fight was to last for five days and four nights while the paratroop battalion from Waalhaven tried in vain to battle its way through the streets to get to them.

It was the morning of 13 May before Major-General Hubicki's 9th Panzer Division finally reached the Moerdijk bridge and rolled across it, cheered by its haggard defenders. The Panzers raced on through Dordrecht, and that evening they clattered into the outskirts of Rotterdam south of the Maas. Among the shattered houses near the southern end of the Willems Bridge, they ground to a halt, pinned down by heavy artillery fire. The paratroops were clinging bitterly to their tenuous foothold on the northern end of the bridge. Their losses had been heavy, and the survivors were exhausted. They had been in action continuously for nearly four days, but there was no question of withdrawing across the bullet-swept bridge to where the Panzers were waiting.

Command of the German forces in Rotterdam now rested on the shoulders of General Rudolf Schmidt, of the 39th Army Corps. His orders were to avoid unnecessary casualties among the Dutch civilians at all costs. On the evening of 13 May he therefore called on the Dutch commander, Colonel Scharoo, to surrender, pointing out that further resistance would lead to widespread damage in the city and would only delay the inevitable capitulation by a few hours. Every one of those hours could represent a disaster in its own way to the German timetable. General von Küchler, c-in-c of the Eighteenth Army, feared that the British were on the point of landing an expeditionary force in Holland. Moreover, the Dutch had to be broken quickly, for the German forces already committed against them were desperately needed for the push through Belgium into northern France.

At 19.00 on 13 May, von Küchler therefore ordered that resistance in Rotterdam was to be smashed by every available means. The battle-plan envisaged a tank attack across the Willems Bridge at 15.30 the following afternoon, preceded by a large-scale air raid on the surrounding area to soften up the defenders. By the morning of the 14th, the Dutch commander still had not replied to General Schmidt's call for surrender. Two German envoys had been flown into the city to discuss capitulation terms; finally, at noon, they managed to get in touch with Colonel Scharoo and delivered their ultimatum – surrender or suffer the destruction of the city centre by the Luftwaffe. Scharoo found himself unable to make the decision alone. He told the envoys that he would have to get in touch with The Hague for further instructions. Half an hour later, the Dutch government replied that it was sending a delegation to Rotterdam to talk terms with the Germans.

The deputation was due to arrive at 14.00. At 13.30 General Schmidt sent a signal to Luftflotte 2 calling off the impending air attack, due to begin at 15.00. He was too late. At 13.25 a hundred Heinkel 111s of KG54 had taken off from their airfields near Bremen. By the time Schmidt's signal reached Luftflotte 2, they were already approaching the Dutch border, and by the time the order to abort the raid got through to KG54's HQ, the Heinkels were already inside Dutch territory. This meant that the radio operator in each aircraft had now closed down his position to take up his combat station behind the machine-gun in the blister beneath the fuselage.

The HE 111s thundered towards Rotterdam in two waves.

One, led by Colonel Lackner, the OC KG54, approached from the east; the other, headed by Lieutenant-Colonel Hohne, commander of 1/KG54, made a wide detour to attack from the south-west. Strapped to his knee, each bomber pilot had a map of the city, with the Dutch-held zones at either end of the bridges outlined in red. It was precisely within these sectors that the pilots had to place their bombs. At 15.05 Lackner's formation roared in over the outskirts of the city from the south, sailing through clusters of flak bursts. Lackner screwed up his eyes and searched for the target along the line of the river, which curved through Rotterdam in a wide loop. It was hard to see anything at all. The city was shrouded in a veil of dusty haze and smoke through which the sun, away to the left, glared with a piercing radiance. It was hardly surprising that the pilots never saw the red flares, the abort signal, which the German ground forces were firing in desperation.

The Heinkels flew over the island in the middle of the Maas and unloaded their bombs in the centre of the Altstadt where the Dutch artillery was in position, then wheeled to starboard and vanished in the haze. A few seconds later, Hohne's formation came in from the south-west. In the cockpit of his Heinkel, Hohne concentrated on following the instructions of his bombardier as the latter guided him in to his target, where fires could be seen blazing fiercely amid piles of rubble. Just as the bombardier pressed the release, Hohne caught an elusvie glimpse of light over the Maas island. Straining his eyes he saw it again, a red flare. He immediately pulled the Heinkel round in a 180-degree turn, and the other pilots followed him, their bombs still on board. Fifty-seven out of the hundred Heinkels of KG54, those of the first wave, and Hohne's own aircraft had dropped a total of a hundred tons of bombs on Rotterdam, pulverizing the city centre. Fire swept through the shattered streets, consuming everything in its path. A great pillar of smoke rose into the afternoon sky, darkening the sun. Beneath it lay the bodies of 814 Dutch civilians.

At 17.00 just two hours after the attack, the Dutch garrison surrendered. At 19.00 the Panzers rolled across the Maas bridges towards the north. The airborne troops, who had held the bridges for so long, watched silently as the monsters clattered by. They were too exhausted even to raise a cheer.

The virtual collapse of Dutch resistance on the 10th meant that the full weight of the German offensive could now be turned on the French Seventh Army, advance units of which had moved into Holland across the Belgian frontier several hours after the start of the German air offensive. On the left flank, the French 68th Division had moved up to occupy the coastline as far as Knokke on the shoulder of the Scheldt estuary, while the 60th, under Colonel Deslaurens, moved towards the estuary itself. The three Dutch ports on the south side of the estuary, Walsoorden, Terneuzen and Breskens, were occupied on the morning of the 10th by reconnaissance groups of the 4th, 9th and 21st Divisions under General Beauchesne and in the afternoon they moved over to Walcheren Island, from where they intended to push on eastwards to join the Dutch Infantry Regiment which had been sent by sea from Dunkirk to Flushing with supporting artillery and orders to secure the narrow neck of land connecting South Beveland with the mainland at Bergen-op-Zoom. The commander of the 68th Division's 224th Regiment, General Durand, however, failed to carry out this task, and his troops – assembled at Walcheren with their small fleet of support craft off shore – suffered considerably from the attentions of German dive-bombers.

In the meantime, on the right flank, advance units of General Sciard's I Corps and the armoured cars of the 6th Cuirassiers from the 1st Light Armoured Division crossed the Antwerp canal as it was getting dark on 10 May and pushed out patrols towards Driessen, Tilburg and Breda. The following morning, two battalions of the 25th Motorized Division moved up to reinforce defensive positions at Breda; one of them reached the town successfully and moved into its positions, but the other was caught in the open by enemy dive-bombers and lost several vehicles, two-thirds of its signalling equipment and two hundred men killed and wounded. The remainder of the battalion straggled into Breda, where they helped to set up a defensive line along the Marck River. In the evening, they were joined on their right flank by advance units of the 9th Motorized Division, while General Beauchesne's units, occupying the ports on the south of the Scheldt estuary, moved up to occupy Bergen-op-Zoom.

On the morning of 12 May, two successive attempts were made by the French to capture the Moerdijk Bridge, first by the 6th Cuirassiers and then by General Beauchesne's units. Both attempts failed and the attackers fell back to consolidate on a line north of the Breda/Bergen road. By noon on the 13th, it was apparent that General Gamelin's plan to relieve the hard-pressed Dutch forces had failed. Moreover, General Billotte, who had just resumed responsibility for co-ordinating the operations of the Belgian Army, the British Expeditionary Force and Army Group One, advised General Giraud that the Seventh Army would soon be called upon to take part in the battle further south and that preparations should be made for the transfer of some divisions.

Later that afternoon, Giraud issued orders for the forces round Breda to begin withdrawing. At first this went well, but then German forces moved up with lightning speed and surrounded a full battalion, which surrendered the following day after it ran out of ammunition. On the morning of the 14th, following the collapse of Dutch resistance in Rotterdam, the spearheads of the 9th Panzer Division fell upon the 25th Motorized Division, which was in full retreat from Breda, throwing the French column into confusion. The Panzers drove on to surround Bergen-op-Zoom where they captured the remnants of the 4th Division Reconnaissance Group and pushed back the 92nd Infantry Regiment south of Woensdrecht, opening the way for the German armour to push along the road leading to South Beveland and Walcheren. In an attempt to plug the gap, General Fagalde quickly brought up the 21st Division to occupy the southern shore of the Scheldt estuary between Walsoorden and Antwerp.

In the early afternoon, General Giraud was ordered to bring

the whole of the Seventh Army to new positions south of Antwerp, where the divisions dug in and prepared for a further move towards the south. During the night of 14/15 May, French forces on South Beveland, principally the 271st Infantry Regiment of the 60th Division, were in full retreat towards Walcheren. Only about three hundred men, however, reached the island, the remainder being trapped and mopped up by the rapidly-advancing Germans. The remaining French forces concentrated on Walcheren, where the French Navy launched a large-scale evacuation. By midnight on the 17th, French resistance on Walcheren was at an end. The Germans were probing into the burning town of Flushing, the 60th French Division had lost almost the whole of the 271st Infantry Regiment, together with the divisional commander, General Deslaurens, who was killed on the quayside, while the 68th Division had lost two battalions and one artillery group. To all intents and purposes, the Seventh Army had ceased to exist as a fighting force, and the battle for Holland was over.

CHAPTER 3

The Ardennes and Northern France, 10 - 16 May

Ever since the days of the Roman Empire, the mighty River Meuse has formed one of western Europe's principal defensive waterways, standing like a barrier between the fertile plains of France, Belgium and Holland and the threat of invasion from the east. From its source near Langres, in the Haute-Marne, its course runs through France and the Low Countries, where it becomes the Maas and divides into two branches, one entering the Rhine above Rotterdam and the other the Hollandisch Diep in the north-east. Through French territory it follows a northerly course until it reaches Stenay, where it veers to the north-west past Sedan and Mézières before turning north again to Givet on the Franco-Belgian border. Flowing northwards to Namur, it then veers once again, this time north eastwards to Liège. Beyond that it flows past Maastricht on the Dutch-Belgian border before sweeping on westwards through the Netherlands towards the sea.

This broad, sleepy, slow-moving river is inextricably mixed with the fighting history of France, flowing above places whose names stand out from the holocaust of the First World War : Verdun, Sedan, Mézières, Liège. It was on the Meuse in 1914 that French troops succeeded in repulsing several German attacks before retreating to the Aisne, and it was on the Meuse again that the pride of the French Army bled in the mud of Verdun and Saint-Mihiel. Finally, it was towards the Meuse in November 1918 that the allied armies turned in their tremendous drive that ended with the capitulation of Germany.

From the strategic point of view, the most important sector of the Meuse defences was at the extreme western end of the

Maginot Line, where the river ran parallel to the Franco-Belgian frontier to the south of the Ardennes. After its northern swing at Mézières, the river continued along the frontier until it reached Givet at the apex of a small peninsula of French territory jutting into Belgium. At this point it swung away from the frontier, flowing through Belgian territory past Dinant, Namur and Liège, running along the western flank of the Ardennes. It was also of vital importance as a frontier defence in Holland, where it ran close to the Dutch-German border beyond Maastricht, flowing past Venlo in the direction of Nijmegen before curving westwards towards the sea.

In May 1940 the French army had the task of defending a ninety-mile stretch of the Meuse, roughly from Sedan to Namur in Belgium. On the extreme left the plan called for the Ninth Army's II and XI Corps to move up into Belgium to consolidate this defensive line from Givet to the Namur forts. The initial task of securing the river line fell to the mechanized brigades of the Ninth Army's two cavalry divisions, the 4th and the 1st, which moved up on 10 May. After the river had been secured, this force was then to move eastwards to join the Belgian frontier forces and delay the German advance for long enough to allow the French infantry divisions to complete the occupation of the left bank of the river.

On the 1st Cavalry's right, the 2nd Moroccan and 2nd Algerian Regiments were to cross the Meuse at Mézières and join up with cavalry units of the Second Army. The leading echelons of the infantry divisions began to move up towards the Meuse by motor transport at noon on the 10th, the main bulk following that evening. Shortly before midnight the vanguard of the 5th Motorized Division reached the river, and the majority of the infantry units were in position by nightfall on the 11th. The left of the division took up position inside the ring formed by the Namur forts between St Heribert and Dave. Two regiments were dug in on the banks of the Meuse itself, with a third – the 39th Infantry Regiment – held as reserve.

The move had gone off relatively smoothly, and the troops had the benefit of full supporting divisional artillery. It was a different story with the 18th Division, two battalions of which, drawn from the 66th and 77th regiments, were to occupy a nine-mile stretch of the river between Anhée and Hastière. The troops reached their positions without too much trouble, but their horse-drawn artillery batteries became hopelessly entangled on the winding roads, where they encountered streams of Belgian refugees, and until the mess could be sorted out, the troops were left with only the 75-mm cannon of the 308th Artillery Regiment to provide supporting fire. A battalion of the 39th Infantry Regiment was hurriedly moved up to strengthen the left flank of the 66th.

Snags too attended the movement of XI Corps's 22nd Division, two battalions of which – from the 19th Regiment – were occupying Givet. On 10 May both these battalions were to move along the river as far as Hastière, where they were to make contact with the advance elements of the 18th Division. The 22nd Division's other two regiments, the 62nd and 119th, were already in position to the south-west near Rumigny and Liart, and detachments of both units were ordered to take up positions on the river between Vireux-Molhain and Givet. However, both regiments were involved in an exercise when the alarm went up, and as a consequence they did not reach the river for another thirty-six hours. More serious still, the division's anti-tank guns, engaged in firing practice at Sissonne, never arrived at all.

On the night of 10/11 May, the 2nd Moroccan and 2nd Algerian Regiments crossed the river and drove on to effect the link with the Second Army's cavalry. The advance proceeded more cautiously when, in the afternoon of the 10th, the cavalry encountered German reconnaissance parties who were scouting ahead of von Kluge's Fourth Army advancing into Belgium south of the Liège-Namur line. The Fourth Army consisted of three corps, V, VIII and II with General Hoth's XV Panzer Corps with its two armoured divisions in support; the 5th Armoured under von Hartlieb advancing on the right and Rommel's 7th advancing on the left. The 7th Panzer had raced across northern Luxembourg unmolested until it reached

Montleban, where it encountered elements of the 3rd Chasseurs Ardennais. These were rapidly destroyed, and the division raced on, reaching Chabreleix on the 10th. The following morning, after the vanguard of the 7th Panzer crossed the River Ourthe, a few shots were exchanged with the French cavalry screen, and at midday Rommel received orders to halt at Marche a few miles further on, in order to let the French build-up on the right bank of the Meuse continue. The idea was to cut off the bulk of French forces with their backs to the river, and destroy them. Because of bridge demolition and a skirmish with the Belgian 2nd Cavalry Division, the 5th Panzer, coming up on Rommel's right, had made slower progress, but its spear-head, led by Colonel Werner, drew level with the 7th Panzer in the late afternoon of the 11th, its tanks opening fire on a detachment of the French 4th Cavalry Division which was attempting to blow up a bridge at Hotton.

On the morning of 12 May the Ninth Army, in the nick of time, received information that the Second Army's Cavalry was retreating and ordered its own cavalry to withdraw across the Meuse. The 1st Cavalry recrossed at Dinant and Hastière that afternoon; the 4th made the crossing further north just before nightfall, destroying bridges and mining crossroads as they went. That same day Rommel received orders to resume his advance, and in the early afternoon the 7th Panzer, its tanks advancing in two parallel columns, reached the Meuse at Dinant and Houx with the main body of the 5th Panzer some-where to the rear. At 16.30 the French 18th Division, dug in on the left bank of the river at Flavion, spotted the first German armoured cars on the other side of the river, and the bridges at Dinant and Anseremme were immediately blown up by the French sappers. However, further down the river – in the II Corps sector – the Germans almost captured the bridge at Yvoir intact. Officers of the 129th Infantry Regiment, includ-ing their colonel, were inspecting the positioning of demolition charges on the west bank of the river when a group of ar-moured cars came racing up. The AFVs shot up the French officers, killing or wounding all of them before racing on to the bridge. Fortunately the French sappers on the other side realized what was happening and blew the structure, which collapsed into the river taking one of the armoured cars with it.

Elsewhere along the river, the sappers succeeded in demolishing most of their prepared objectives but in many cases the damage caused to most of the bridges was relatively superficial. Added to the fact that the Belgians had omitted to make any preparations for demolition, there was a critical shortage of explosives, and the sappers found it hard to do their work effectively. To make matters worse, the Belgians had left large numbers of boats and barges on the east bank of the river, and although French artillery made some attempt to destroy them, the majority fell intact into the hands of the Germans.

In the early hours of 13 May, the northernmost of 7th Panzer's two spearheads, led by Colonel Fürst, arrived on the Meuse at Houx. To their astonishment, the Germans found that both the lock and the weir at Houx Island were unguarded. In the mist and darkness, Rommel's motor-cycle troops passed across the weir unmolested, and by daybreak they were in position on the high ground on the other side of the Meuse. The 5th Panzer's spearhead meanwhile, led by Colonel Werner, had attempted to cross the river at Yvoir, only to find the bridge there blown. Werner consequently moved on to Houx, arriving shortly after Rommel's force and pushing over his motor-cycle troops to attack north-westwards against the French 129th Infantry Regiment. The right flank of the 129th was to be protected by a battalion of the 39th Regiment. Because the bank of the Meuse was virtually indefensible, being flat and open, the 39th took up positions about half a mile from the river on the wooded slopes of the hills. The commander of the 129th was not aware of this, and when Werner's troops attacked from the right direction, he came to the conclusion that the 39th had been either overwhelmed or forced to retreat. The French were unable to stand the German advance. A counter-attack by a battalion of the 14th Dragoons was quickly shrivelled up, and the reserve battalion of the

129th, rushed up from Bioul, was subjected to heavy Stuka attacks and was not able to go into action until late afternoon.

With the coming of daylight and the lifting of the early morning mist, the advance guard of Rommel's 7th Panzer found itself pinned down on the wooded slopes of the Meuse's west bank by highly accurate fire from the 18th Division's artillery, which prevented more reinforcements from using the crossing at Houx. When the Germans attempted to push forward, they met stiff resistance from the 66th Infantry Regiment, dug in on a line running through the woods. The southernmost of the 7th Panzer's spearheads, meanwhile, led by Colonel von Bismarck, had run into trouble while attempting to cross the Meuse near Dinant where the French had blown up a vital bridge. The German shock troops did succeed in crossing the river in rubber boats between Leffe and Bouvignes, but they were hopelessly pinned down by the French defenders who, well dug in on the steep bank of the Meuse, kept up continuous small arms fire until several German heavy tanks arrived and opened up a heavy barrage from the opposite bank. Under the cover of this the Germans reinforced their bridgehead on the west bank, gradually pushing the French back, but little progress was made until the night of 13/14 May when some of the lighter tanks were ferried across.

The news that the Germans had succeeded in forcing a crossing of the Meuse at Houx came as a considerable shock to the staff officers in Ninth Army headquarters at Vervins. The word came less than an hour after General Billotte called at Ninth Army HQ and expressed his anxiety to General Corap about the morale of the troops of General Huntziger's Second Army, who were said to be in a state of near panic over the news of the German breakthrough.

In the small hours of 12/13 May the bulk of the 18th Infantry Division began to arrive on the Meuse supported by their crucial artillery. Part of this force made a small counterattack across the river at 18.30 on the afternoon of the 13th, with a group of Hotchkiss tanks pushing ahead for about half a mile and taking a few prisoners. However the supporting infantry, which were to have been drawn from the 39th Regiment, failed to arrive, and without them the tanks had to abandon the attack and return across the Meuse.

For the Germans, speed was of the essence. Realizing this, General von Kleist strongly advocated that his Panzers be allowed to force a passage of the Meuse immediately, without waiting for the full support of the infantry. At midnight on the 12th, he called General Heinz Guderian to his command post and ordered him to be ready to launch xix Armoured Corps across the Meuse at 16.00 on the following day. The attack was to be carried out at Sedan with the 2nd, 1st and 10th Panzer Divisions deployed from west to east and storming the river in a concerted three-pronged thrust. By nightfall on the 12th, it was clear that the French were rapidly losing the battle to reach the Meuse in strength before the Germans did. As darkness fell, many of Corap's troops were still moving northwards along the narrow roads towards the river, where their positions were still unmanned, harassed continually by the Luftwaffe.

On the north of the Ninth Army's front, south of Namur, the 5th Motorized Division under General Boucher was in place, as was General Vauthier's 61st Infantry Division and the 102nd Garrison Division. It was in the critical central sector running from Dinant to Vireux that the advance remained woefully weak. The troops expected to hold this twenty-mile stretch of territory were the reservists of General Martin's xi Corps, comprising the 18th Infantry Division and 22nd Infantry Division. By nightfall on the 12th, five battalions of the 18th had arrived, and the remainder were still struggling along the roads to the rear. In the Second Army's sector, the position was even worse, principally because General Huntziger had decided to reshuffle his divisions at the last minute. On 10 May for example, x Corps consisted of the 55th Infantry Division on the left and the 3rd North African Division on the right. However, Huntziger decided towards the end of the day to increase the size of the Corps by bringing up the reserve

71st Infantry Division from Vouzier, thirty miles to the rear. The 71st did not arrive until the evening of the 12th, and in its efforts to take up positions between the 55th and 3rd Divisions, it succeeded only in disrupting the stability of the entire front.

To the east of Sedan, between the town and the fortifications of the Maginot Line, lay the Second Army's xvIII Corps under General Rochard, in position along the River Chiers and for the time being under no direct pressure from the German attack. It was ironic that the xvIII Corps consisted of two of the Second Army's best divisions, the 3rd Colonial and the 41st. It was ironic too that to the west of xvIII Corps, on the vulnerable junction of the Ninth and Second Armies between Sedan and Mézières, Corap and Huntziger had placed four of their weakest divisions, the 61st Infantry, the 102nd Garrison and the Second Army's 55th and 71st Infantry Divisions, all fortress troops with no conception of mobile warfare and little battle-worthiness.

Against this tenuous line were massed on the night of 12/13 May no fewer than five Panzer divisions, the three comprising General Guderian's xix Armoured Corps and Reinhardt's 6th and 8th opposite Monthermé, facing the centre of the Ninth Army's xli Corps. Further to the north, the 5th and 7th Panzer Divisions of General Hoth's xv Corps were also beginning to assemble for a thrust against the French xi Corps sector around Dinant. Behind the German armour and shock troops poised for the assault, the roads leading towards the Meuse and Sedan presented an almost unbelievable sight to the German crews climbing away on their missions in the spreading dawn of 13 May. Packed nose to tail, churning slowly forward, was the mightiest concentration of armour in the history of warfare; fifteen hundred tanks moving in three great phalanxes. The whole column was a hundred miles long, and behind it, still deep inside Germany, came the infantry divisions whose task it would be to consolidate the ground won by the initial thrust of the Panzers.

For the allied air forces this enormous mass of men and

material represented the target of a lifetime, but as the hours
dragged on, still no orders came to unleash the allied bombers.
In the joint HQ at Chauny, Air Marshal Barratt, commanding
the British Air Forces in France, and General d'Astier de la
Vigerie, commanding the Northern Zone of Air Operations,
paced up and down in frustration as they awaited the necessary signal from the French GHQ. Their anger mounted when,
at 08.00, they received a signal restricting allied air operations
to fighter and reconnaissance activity. At that very moment
the enemy columns, jammed tightly along the narrow roads
through the Ardennes, were highly vulnerable to air attack,
and yet because of the French terror of Luftwaffe reprisals and
the totally irrational hope of General Gamelin that a bombing
war might somehow be avoided, the opportunity to hit the
invaders hard was being thrown away.

Despite all the indications to the contrary, the French still
expected that it would take the Germans several days to build
up their assault. In fact the greatest activity appeared to be
developing in the sector held by General Rochard's XVIII Corps,
holding the line of the River Chiers, where the rumble of tank
engines could be heard continuously through the morning
mist. Then at 07.00 French outposts reported a massive movement of German troops down through the woods along almost
the whole front, the movement apparently channelled towards
Sedan, Balan and Bazeilles. Most of the German troops were
red-eyed through lack of sleep, exhausted after their long
forced marches through the Ardennes and soaked through by
the dripping vegetation in the forest. Nevertheless, there was
to be no respite for them; the momentum of the German
assault could not be allowed to falter.

During the morning of the 13th, which dawned bright and
sunny with a few shreds of mist clinging over the Meuse and
the woods on either side, the heavy artillery of the French X
and XVIII Corps opened up on river crossing points, strategic
road junctions and the approaches to the Meuse. By midday,
however, there was a critical shortage of ammunition. Apart
from the general confusion that existed, fresh supplies coming

up from the rear were subjected to incessant air attacks by the Luftwaffe. It later transpired that requests for further supplies of ammunition sent through urgently to HQ Second Army had never arrived or, if they had, had been ignored. During the morning of 13 May, the Luftwaffe struck the French posts on the Meuse in relatively small numbers, the forward positions being attacked by groups of up to six Stukas and medium bombers. In the afternoon, however, the full weight of Fliegerkorps II and VIII was suddenly turned on the real pivot of the battle in support of the armoured thrust at Sedan by the XIX and XXI Army Corps. Luftwaffe orders were to pin down the French defences while the German ground forces established a bridgehead. This was to be achieved by relatively small formations of aircraft – notably Stukas – attacking in relays, rather than by a single all-out air attack.

The first phase unrolled on schedule at 16.00 hours on 13 May with a highly effective precision attack by Junkers 87s of Stuka-Geschwader 77 on French artillery emplacements on the west bank of the Meuse. This was followed within minutes by a second raid, this time by the Dornier 17s of Kampfgeschwader 2 – and so it went on for hours on end, with successive waves of bombers droning over the river, unloading their sticks with deadly accuracy, and turning for home in almost leisurely manner. The French fighters tore gaps in their ranks, but more often than not, the highly effective Messerschmitt escort prevented the French fighter groups from coming anywhere near the bomber formations. The total number of sorties flown by the Luftwaffe in the day's operations was about seven hundred, including 310 by the Dornier 17s and Heinkel 111s of KGS 2, 3 and 53, and two hundred by the Junkers 87 of StGs 2 and 77.

Further north, the assault on the Meuse at Houx and Dinant by General Hoth's XV Panzer Corps was supported by the Junkers 87s of StG 1 and the Dornier 17s of KG 76 and 77. For the defending French troops, the air attacks were a nightmare. Most of the French air-raid shelters were only half completed and afforded hardly any protection from the onslaught. Even before the air attack was over, four brigades of German 105-mm guns opened up a heavy fire on the French x Corps sector. Under cover of the bombardment, the German infantry, consisting of the 1st Rifle Regiment of the 1st Panzer Division, commanded by Colonel Balck, and the Grossdeutschland Infantry Regiment attached to xix Panzer Corps, launched themselves across the Meuse on river boats and rafts, sheltered to some extent by the vast cloud of dust and smoke that swirled across the river from the bombing on the opposite bank,

Dazed and bewildered, the French defenders began to emerge from their shelters to be confronted by the first waves of German shock troops, storming up the river bank towards them. One by one the French positions collapsed under the relentless pressure, many of them being taken from the rear by the rapidity of the German thrust. Shortly after 18.00, ten batteries of x Corps artillery fell intact into German hands. They had been abandoned by their crews as soon as German troops approached to within half a mile. While 1st Panzer's assault troops and the independent Grossdeutschland Regiment went ashore at Gaulier to the west of Sedan, 10th Panzer's assault group – the 69th and 86th Rifle Battalions – stormed the river banks at Wadelincourt, to the south-east of the town. Progress was slow here, for the air attacks and shelling had not succeeded in destroying many of the defensive bunkers, and these put up a heavy machine-gun fire against the attackers.

The main problem here was the lack of artillery support, and flanking fire from the Maginot Line south of Curignan had been particularly worrying. There were delays, too, in the assault of the 2nd Panzer Divisions, which was to have stormed the Meuse at Donchéry to the west of Sedan. In fact, only the advance elements of 2nd Panzer, the reconnaissance battalion and the motor-cycle battalion, together with the Division's heavy artillery, saw action on 13 May, and these did not succeed in forcing a crossing. Most of the Division's tanks in fact were still on the Samois River and would not arrive until after dark. These setbacks however were more than compensated for by the rapid thrust of the 1st Panzer Division. By nightfall the German assault troops had torn their way through the French defences in the Marfée Wood region, two miles inland from Sedan. By midnight the Division's rifle brigade was pushing on towards Chéhéry and Bulson, while a battalion of the Grossdeutschland Regiment cleared the area between Wadelincourt and Ennemane.

At Gaulier, xix Corps engineers constructed a bridge across the river, enabling the 2nd Panzer Division to begin moving across at dawn, the tanks rolling past literally thousands of French prisoners herded into pockets along the river banks. Since the Luftwaffe would not be able to lend its full support to the battle on the Meuse during 14 May, its bombers being needed elsewhere, it was vital that the Germans got as much armour as possible over to the left bank to meet an anticipated French counter-attack. This developed at 07.00 that morning, with the French 213th Infantry Regiment and a company of the 7th Tank Battalion from the direction of Connage. It was a gallant attempt but it was pitifully weak and was doomed to failure. Less than an hour after setting out, the French ran headlong into the tanks of the 1st Panzer Division. In the brief, one-sided battle that followed, the Tank Battalion lost eleven of its fifteen Hotchkiss light tanks.

The lightning speed and the relentless push of the German attack threw the French into total confusion. Frantic troops streamed back from the front with wild reports of masses of German armour converging on the French posts from all sides. Panic swept through the whole of the 55th and 71st Divisions, and the trickle of men abandoning their positions quickly became a flood. The rout began in fact even before the first German tanks crossed the Meuse on the 13th. The total breakdown of morale spread throughout all sectors like an inferno and could not be stopped. Corps and Divisional HQs, their lines of communication with the front shattered by the German bombing, were incapable of exercising the slightest control over the surging hysteria. On the morning of 14 May, the roads leading back from the Meuse were crammed with struggling columns of French troops, officers and men alike. In their haste to get away, they abandoned well-prepared defences, artillery batteries, rifles, webbing, sometimes even boots. The whole of the 55th Infantry Division's positions were abandoned; the only divisional unit that still remained more or less intact was part of the 331st Infantry Regiment, which held on to its positions on the River Bar supported by several batteries of 75-mm artillery.

The German attack meanwhile maintained its impetus. In the early afternoon of 14 May, General Guderian ordered the 1st and 2nd Panzer Divisions to strike westwards across the River Bar, leaving the 10th Panzer Division and the Grossdeutschland Regiment to cover the invasion's southern flank. The 2nd Panzer Division crossed the Meuse near Donchéry and battled its way up the southern bank, its forward elements racing on to capture Villers-sur-Bar, while the bulk of the Division continued to cross the river in an uninterrupted flood. At the same time, the remainder of the 1st Panzer crossed the river at Omicourt and pushed on westwards, by-passing Vendresse in a pincer movement. The 2nd Panzer also split up in a two-pronged thrust, mopping up what remained of the French 55th Division and capturing Dom-le-Mesnil. The German commanders could hardly believe their good fortune. Not only had they succeeded in capturing many vital bridges across the Meuse intact but the French long range artillery in the Maginot Line and its westerly extension had not laid down the weight of fire that had been expected. If this had been the case, the German advance might have quickly become bogged down.

At daybreak on 13 May, while the left flank of the Ninth Army fought against the German thrust through the Belgian Ardennes and x Corps of the Second Army crumbled rapidly under the German battering-ram at Sedan, the formation that stood at the centre of the allied line, General Libaud's XLI Corps, guarding the Meuse from Vireux to Anchamps, had yet to feel the weight of the German attack. The principal reason for this was that General Reinhardt's XLI Panzer Corps, which was detailed to attack in this area, had been compelled to pause to allow Guderian's divisions to swing southwards ahead of it. Also, the roads leading to the Meuse in this area, passing through southern Belgium and Luxembourg, were practically non-existent, which slowed down German progress considerably. It was not until the night of 10/11 May that Reinhardt's armour began to move, with XLI Corps's two divisions – the 8th and 6th Panzer – proceeding in column through the forest towards the Meuse.

As yet, the French had no indication where the blow would fall. The first inkling came soon after dawn on 13 May, when the Luftwaffe carried out a heavy divebombing attack on positions held by the 42nd Malgache Demi-Brigade, a colonial machine-gun unit of the 102nd Fortress Division, half of whose personnel were from Madagascar. The 42nd had the task of defending a section of the line in front of Monthermé, a town lying on a spur of land jutting into a loop of the River Meuse at its junction with the Semois. The air attack continued for five hours. It was watched by men of the 61st Division, holding an area of high ground further to the west of the Meuse, whose own positions remained untouched. When the last of the bombers droned away, the 61st division's observers saw a long line of enemy motor transport, including artillery, moving southwards along the Monthermé road. The Division's artillery opened up but the range was too great, and the German advance continued unimpeded.

The Monthermé position itself was defended by the 42nd Demi-Brigade's 2nd Battalion, consisting of three machine-gun companies. No. 4 Company was dug in on the banks of the river loop that flowed round the spur of land on which Monthermé was perched; No. 5 was situated in a line across the neck of the spur itself, and No. 6 was in place at Chateau-Regnault, further to the south and behind the main line of defence. Minutes after the air bombardment ceased, the Germans brought up a number of self-propelled guns, which opened up a withering and highly accurate fire on the French positions. Under cover of this, the German assault troops began to cross the river in rafts and rubber boats, threading their

way through streams of machine-gun bullets that churned up
the water around them. Hitting the opposite bank, they raced
through the gaps torn in the French defences by the air attack
and artillery bombardment, working their way rapidly towards
the French positions on the crest of the spur. Once in position
there, they were able to attack the remaining French defences
on the river line from the rear, pouring down fire from the
high ground. In less than an hour, the French 5th Company
had been annihilated, and the Germans pressed on along the
spur towards the point where the 4th Company sat astride it.
The French here put up a better resistance, withdrawing only
when pressure became insupportable. They re-grouped on the
exit of the spur and launched a fierce counter-attack that
brought the Germans to a temporary halt.

After dark the French resistance was further strengthened
by the arrival of the reserve of the 61st Division, comprising
two battalions of the 248th Infantry Regiment, which established themselves in support of what was left of the 4th
Company. The Germans renewed their attack shortly after
07.00 on the 14th. They tried three times to dislodge the
French defenders, and each time the attacks were shrivelled up
by a storm of French machine-gun fire. The French, however,
also suffered badly, and by late afternoon both sides were practically exhausted. The stalemate was broken at 19.00, when
the Luftwaffe returned and blasted the 4th Company's positions
into smoking rubble. The German troops attacked again through
the dust and smoke, and this time they succeeded in breaking
through the French centre, engaging the defenders in a desperate hand to hand fight with sub-machine-guns, bayonets, boots
and fists. Ten minutes later it was all over. The remnants of
the 4th Company were hurled back, and the Germans paused
to regroup.

During the night, the French made a further attempt to
establish a new line of resistance half a mile to the rear, but
at dawn the following morning, the men once again found
themselves cowering against the earth as the Stukas wheeled
and dived overhead. This time the Germans had armoured

support, and as the air attack petered out, the tanks moved up, rolling through the French barbed wire and past the bodies that sprawled in their foxholes, torn apart by blast or bomb fragments. Ninety minutes later, the 42nd Demi-Brigade had ceased to exist, its HQ surrounded and its commander taken prisoner.

The speed of the German thrust across the Meuse had been facilitated not only by the capture of several strategic bridges intact but by the efficiency with which the German engineers had thrown pontoons across the river. In the early hours of the 14th, General Billotte, commanding the French Army Group One, telephoned Air Marshal Barratt, commander of the British Air Forces in France, and begged him to send the Advanced Air Striking Force into action in the Sedan area. 'Victory or defeat hinges on the destruction of those bridges', the French General emphasized. Barratt accordingly authorized the AASF to attack the pontoons across the Meuse, and the first two missions of this kind, carried out at 04.30 and 06.30 by two flights of Fairey Battle light bombers drawn from Nos 103 and 150 Squadrons in the Gaulier sector, were encouraging; all the bombers returned safely to base. A few of the pontoons appeared to have been damaged, but Guderian's Panzers continued to rumble across into the bridgehead established on the west bank the previous evening, while further north the 6th Panzer Division pushed through the second breach at Monthermé, and in the Dinant sector Rommel's 7th Panzers poured into the third bridgehead.

During the morning and early afternoon, the French threw all their available bombers against these objectives, including the elderly Amiot 143s which had hitherto been restricted to night bombing operations. The French bombers were shot to ribbons by the flak and prowling Messerschmitts, and by noon on the 14th there were no reserves left. Up to this moment, Air Vice Marshal Playfair, following Air Marshal Barratt's instructions, had been holding the AASF in reserve to give his squadrons a few more hours in which to scrape together their available resources. These amounted to only sixty-two Battles

and eight Blenheims, but with the French bomber forces in-
effective, Barratt and Playfair had no alternative but to commit
these battered remnants. Between 15.00 and 16.00 that afternoon, the AASF threw into the cauldron every aircraft that
could still fly. It was a massacre. No. 12 Squadron lost four
aircraft out of five; No. 142 four out of eight; No. 226 three
out of six; No. 105 six out of eleven; No. 150 lost all four;
No. 88 one out of ten; No. 103 three out of eight and No. 218
ten out of eleven. Of the eight Blenheims sent out by 114 and
139 Squadrons, only three returned to base. It was the highest
loss in an operation of similar size ever experienced by the RAF
– and all that was achieved was the destruction of two pontoon
bridges and the damaging of two more. At dusk the pontoons
were again attacked by twenty-eight Blenheims of No. 2
Group, operating from Britain. Seven aircraft failed to return.

On the morning of 15 May the allied commanders began to
realize for the first time the full seriousness of the situation.
Everywhere along the front the allies were suffering reverses.
In the north the Dutch were shattered, their last pockets of
resistance being mopped up by the men of von Küchler's
Eighteenth Army. In Belgium, von Reichenau's Sixth Army
had hurled the Belgians back from their forward posts and
were now pushing Prioux's Cavalry Corps back towards the
Gembloux Gap. In this sector at least there was still some
hope, for in their drive towards the sea, the Sixth Army would
soon encounter the divisions of the French First Army – which
numbered some of the finest fighting men France possessed –
flanked on the north by the incomparable troops of the British
Expeditionary Force. Here at least there was a possibility that
the German drive might be checked.

On the Meuse it was a different story. Hour by hour the
situation grew increasingly hopeless. News of the German
breakthrough at Sedan seemed to have stupefied the French
General Staff. General Georges, in fact, wept openly when he
heard the news. Everything now depended on the ability of
the French to launch an effective counter-offensive. In an effort
to plug the gap, it was decided to bring the 1st Armoured

Division from Charleroi to attack from north to south, to move up the 2nd Armoured Division from Vervins to attack from west to east and to employ the 3rd Armoured Division, which was already in the Second Army's area, to engage the enemy forces at Sedan and attempt to drive them back across the Meuse. As a further measure, six training battalions were sent to occupy a line between Liart and Montcornet and a number of artillery and armoured units were drawn from the general reserve and ordered to concentrate near Lyon, under the command of Colonel Charles de Gaulle. Further north the Ninth Army still retained much of its coherence, but there was little possibility of launching an effective counter-attack in this sector for the troops were hardly in a fit state to hold their existing positions. The troops of General Martin's XI Corps, which arrived at the front on the 13th, had expected to find prepared positions; there were none. Moreover, these ill-trained and ill-equipped reservist troops were now called upon to defend a strip of front through which the enemy had already broken in one place, at Haut-le-Wastia.

At 04.00 in the morning of the 14th, the Germans launched an attack against XI Corps's 129th Infantry Regiment and succeeded in pushing it off the river bank, leaving the flank of its neighbour, the 8th Infantry Regiment, dangerously exposed. The French immediately scraped together some forces for a counter-attack; these consisted of the 14th Regiment of Motorized Dragoons and the 1st Divisional Reconnaissance Group, which were detailed to re-capture Haut-le-Wastia at dawn. The counter-attack enjoyed some initial success, and the French succeeded in overwhelming the German motor-cycle battalion which occupied the village, taking forty prisoners, but because of the speed of the German advance elsewhere, there was a danger that the French force might become isolated and it was withdrawn to the main line of resistance a couple of hours later. Soon afterwards the French line began to yield at two new points, north and south of Houx. At Yvoir German troops were expanding their bridgehead on the west bank of the Meuse, and further south at Dinant in XI Corps's sector Rommel's 7th Panzer

Division, whose engineers had worked throughout the night to repair the broken span of the bridge at Dinant, managed to push thirty tanks across to the west bank at first light to support the infantry.

Rommel's plan was to push straight on through the Philippeville Gap, twenty miles to the west, after clearing the heights on the west bank of the Meuse. These were held by the thinly spaced troops of General Bouffet's 18th Infantry Division, with the 1st Cavalry holding the village of Onhaye to their right. The Germans attacked in strength at dawn, and by the middle of the morning one French position after another was falling before their onslaught. The Panzer spearhead broke through and plunged on towards Onhaye, which fell that afternoon after a bitter fight. Beyond the village the tanks were slowed down for a time by stiff opposition from the 4th North African Division – which, on General Corap's orders, had reached the front after a forced march throughout the night – the 1st Light Cavalry Division and some elements of the crumbling 18th Division. Shortly before nightfall the Germans reached Anthée, three miles beyond Onhaye, where they paused to re-group. Soon afterwards the village was attacked by a battalion of the 25th Algerian Tirailleurs, who succeeded in re-capturing it after a ferocious hand to hand struggle. The success, however, was only a temporary one, for an hour later the Germans counter-attacked and dislodged the Algerians once more.

With the coming of darkness, the 18th Division no longer had a defensive line. On its right flank the other XI Corps division, the 22nd, was in full retreat and except in one place, south of Vireux, had been hurled back from the river line completely. The only hope now lay with speedy intervention by the French 1st Armoured Division, which General Corap had decided to transfer to the Ninth Army in support of the crumbling XI Corps. Two battalions of B.1 tanks, the 28th and 37th, set out from Lambusart north-east of Charleroi in the afternoon of the 14th, but their progress was hampered by fleeing columns of panic-stricken Belgian refugees. It was almost dark by the time the tanks reached a position near

Flavion, about two miles from Anthée, where the Germans were confronted by the 25th Algerians. It was now that the deficiencies of the B.1s became apparent. After their long haul across the Belgian roads, the tanks had fuel for only two hours of operations. They could do nothing but sit tight and await the arrival of the refuelling tanks which were still some distance behind, battling their way across those same roads in company with two battalions of Hotchkiss tanks and six battalions of 105-mm guns.

The collapse of the 18th, 22nd and 61st French Divisions meant that the whole centre of the Ninth Army's line on the Meuse was crumbling between Dinant and Monthermé. Hopes of a counter-attack by the 1st Armoured Division faded when the commander of one of the Hotchkiss battalions, the 26th, reported to General Bruneau, the divisional commander, with the news that his tanks were still fourteen miles from the front and were unable to make progress through crowds of retreating soldiers and refugees. When Bruneau sent a messenger to report this fact to XI Corps HQ, the officer returned and told him that the HQ appeared to have decamped and nobody knew where it had gone. To add to the problems, some of the tanks that did succeed in pushing their way through the congested roads took the wrong turning and became hopelessly lost, scattered all over the countryside.

At 05.00 hours on the morning of the 15th, the 25th Hotchkiss Battalion finally joined the two B1 Battalions near Anthée. The other Hotchkiss battalion, the 26th, seemed to have disappeared from the face of the earth. At about the same time, the Armoured Division's fuel tankers also arrived, together with the supporting artillery of the 5th Chasseurs à Pied and the artillery battery. Bruneau ordered one artillery battalion to go into position near Stave to protect the tanks while they were re-fuelled. The other four battalions he sent to take up positions at Erpion, six miles west of Philippeville, where the Armoured Division had orders to assemble prior to the projected counter-offensive.

The re-fuelling was still going on when suddenly the battery

of 105s opened fire on an unseen target. It was in fact the advance element of Rommel's 7th Panzer, followed by the 5th
Panzer, which had crossed the Meuse during the night and
were now advancing westwards in the direction of Philippeville. The Germans were confident that they would meet little
resistance. Ahead of them there were only scattered remnants
of the 77th and 66th Infantry Divisions, fragments of the 1st
Cavalry and the 4th North African. Rommel had no way of
knowing that behind this crumbling infantry screen, hidden
on the other side of the wooded valley behind Morville, were
the sixty heavy tanks of Bruneau's 1st Armoured Division.
The German column on which the 105-mm battalion had
opened fire, consisting of the 25th Panzer Regiment, raced on
almost unchecked, ignoring the leading tanks of the French
28th Battalion that rolled out of the woods and opened fire.
For five minutes, the two sides blazed away at each other with
everything they had, and several of the French tanks sustained
damage. The German column thundered on and vanished in
the direction of Philippeville in a cloud of dust and diesel
fumes. It was just as well that Rommel had paid no more
attention to the French armour, for if the Germans had investi-
gated more closely, they would have found the 28th Battalion,
its B.1 tanks still immobile through lack of fuel, at their mercy
in the woods. Apart from that, Rommel dared not slacken his
pace. To achieve maximum success, his Panzers had to reach
Philippeville as quickly as possible, sweeping resistance before
him and enabling the remainder of the XV Armoured Corps to
consolidate.

The 1st Armoured Division's good fortune, however, was
not to last. Almost exactly an hour after Rommel's tanks had
raced by, the 31st Panzer Regiment under Colonel Werner
came rolling along the same road, alerted to the presence of
French armour by Rommel's wireless operators. This time
there was to be no escape for the French. Werner immediately
went into the attack using his own heavy armour, 35 Mk IIIs
and 32 Mk IVs with artillery support. The 28th Battalion of
heavy B.1 tanks had still not been re-fuelled, and Werner,

puzzled at their lack of mobility and sensing some kind of trap, set out to outflank the French battalion. In doing so, his heavy armour collided head-on with the light and under-armed Hotchkiss tanks of the French 26th Battalion. What followed was a massacre. Within minutes the bulk of the Hotchkiss tanks had been transformed into shattered, burning hulks. Seeing what had happened, Bruneau ordered one company of the 27th Battalion, with heavy B.1 tanks, to go to the 26th's aid, but it was too late. Only six of the 26th Battalion's Hotchkiss tanks survived the encounter, and the B tanks were annihilated. The same fate overtook the motionless tanks of the 28th, which were overrun and their crews killed or captured. What was left of the 37th Battalion, meanwhile, tried desperately to get away, driving at top speed towards the village of Ermeton-sur-Biert. Anticipating such a move, Werner had sent ahead the anti-tank regiment of the 5th Panzer to lie in wait for the French AFVs. Not one of the French tanks survived. After this action the 1st Armoured Division no longer existed as a fighting force, although its 25th Hotchkiss Battalion, which had been scattered over the countryside the night before, was still intact, as were five batteries of 105-mm guns and a few hundred men of the 5th Chasseurs. Most of these units had finally assembled near Solre-le-Château, although the Hotchkiss Battalion was still lacking two of its companies. The one or two B tanks that had survived had to be abandoned because they ran out of fuel. The surviving Hotchkiss tanks were sent to support troops fighting at various sectors of the front, and most of them were wiped out in subsequent actions.

So ended the brief combat record of the 1st Armoured Division, and with it went the hope for the shattered remnants of XI Corps.

CHAPTER 4

The Collapse in the North, 16 – 21 May

The rapid breakthrough by the German armoured divisions on both sides of Sedan, followed by the progressive collapse of the French Ninth Army, placed the Second Army in a critical position. On the Second Army's front there was a dangerous gap on 14 May caused by the disruption of the 55th Division, and although the 71st Division and 14th Division were both redeployed to meet the new threat, the real danger lay to the west of the River Bar, where the only Second Army troops were one battalion of the 331st Infantry Regiment and two groups of 75-mm artillery drawn from the 55th Division.

The only reserves available to the Second Army at this time were the 5th Cavalry Division and the 1st Cavalry Brigade under the overall command of General Chanoine, which had only just been pulled out of the line after three days' fighting and were virtually exhausted. Nevertheless, the threat was too great for the question of fatigue to be considered, and in the early hours of the 14th General Huntziger ordered Chanoine's group to cross the Ardennes Canal and set up a line of defence along the canal and the Bar river from La Cassine to Saint Aignan, at the same time supporting what was left of the 55th Division as it retreated from the north under relentless enemy pressure. There was some reassurance in the fact that on the Second Army's immediate left, the Ninth Army's XLI Corps on the River Meuse were still intact, although this was now threatened by the enemy foothold on the Monthermé peninsula. In addition there was the German crossing in the Donchéry/Sedan area, which put the right flank of the 102nd Division in danger because all its defences were orientated

1 The days of wine and roses – a contingent of the BEF marches through Paris in the first weeks of the war

2 German tank destroyed by a direct hit, on the approach road to the Western Front

3 The defeated – General Maxime Weygand in June 1940, after the Germans launched their final offensive against the crumbling French armies

4 General Heinz Guderian, whose armoured columns spearheaded the German drive to the channel coast

5 April 1940 – British Bristol Blenheims fly off on reconnaissance

6 German Ju 87B Stuka bombers, which devastated towns and cities throughout northern Europe

7 German bomb damage in Arras, May 1940

8 The whole tragedy of war is reflected in the face of an elderly Belgian refugee

9 Tired men of the BEF return to England

10 Evacuated British troops look back at the Cherbourg supply dumps, burned to prevent them falling into German hands

11 Hastily covered bodies and an abandoned gun pointing ineffectually skywards – mute signs of the Allied retreat to the coast

12 One of the first pictures taken by the Germans when they entered Dunkirk

13 The unlucky ones – British and French prisoners marched away from Dunkirk. The original caption on this (German) photograph reads 'So they march to Berlin, but not as they had imagined!'

14 The final gesture – German troops in Paris parade through the Arc de Triomphe

towards the attack from the east. The German thrust now
threatened its flank and rear.

By the morning of the 14th, the Germans were occupying
the whole south bank of the Meuse between Sedan and the
River Bar and the German armour and infantry were group-
ing in the Bulson/Cheméry area with the 2nd Panzer Division
crossing the river at Donchéry. The second echelon of the 2nd
Panzer also crossed the river at Saint Aignan and had a skirmish with a squadron of tanks from the French 5th Cavalry,
at the conclusion of which they captured the two groups of
75-mms of the 55th Division. The main weight of the 2nd
Panzer's thrust was now directed against the French 148th
Regiment at Dom le Mesnil, which was eventually taken at
14.00 hours. At the conclusion of the battle, two battalions of
the 148th had been annihilated, together with the 239th Infantry Regiment of the 53rd Division. Towards noon the 1st
Panzer Division also crossed the Ardennes Canal at Malmy
and pushed on in two columns towards Singly and Omont,
driving the 5th Cavalry Division and 1st Cavalry Brigade before
it.

The most serious of the Second Army's deficiencies was the
failure of General Huntziger to commit his available armour
at the right place and time. The armoured formation immediately at his disposal was the 3rd Armoured Division, which
had formed in March under the leadership of General Brocard.
Equipped with two battalions of B.1 tanks, the 41st and 49th,
and two of Hotchkiss, the 42nd and 45th, the 3rd Armoured
suffered from a number of serious defects, not the least of
which was that there had been no time to train it properly.
Moreover a number of tanks on its inventory were unservice-
able because of a lack of spare parts, and since there was a
shortage of 1938 model 37-mm guns, the Hotchkiss battalions
still used old 1916 guns of 25-mm calibre which had only half
the range of more modern weapons. In May 1940 the division
was only two-thirds effective and lacked heavy trucks, breakdown equipment, tank transporters and tracked fuel tanks.
The latter was particularly serious since the division's nearest

D

fuel depot was at Sillery near Reims, over a hundred miles from the division's main area of operations. When the Germans attacked, the 3rd Armoured Division's supporting artillery, the 319th Artillery Regiment, was still in the process of formation and the two groups which were operational employed different types of guns which needed different ammunition. The division was also supposed to have an anti-tank battery equipped with 47-mm guns, but this never reached the front. The division's infantry battalion, the 16th Chasseurs à Pied, had only half its planned complement of carriers, and its reconnaissance group was without scout cars or motor-cycles. There was to have been an observation flight equipped with Mureaux 115 aircraft, but although the crews of these arrived, the aircraft themselves failed to materialize. In all, the division was some twenty-three tanks and 270 vehicles below strength.

General Brocard arrived at the Second Army's HQ at Senuc on the morning of 13 May and found a situation of total chaos. It was almost twenty-four hours before he had gleaned sufficient intelligence to enable him to concentrate his division north of the Aisne between Le Chesne and Tourteron, a task which in itself proved incredibly difficult. The assembly was still under way when Brocard received new orders to the effect that his division was to be attached to XXI Corps under the command of General Flavigny. Brocard received the news with a certain sense of relief, for Flavigny was reputed to have a deep understanding of the use of mechanized warfare, coupled with a coolness and clear-cut air of authority qualities which were all too necessary in the present situation. The relief, however, was short lived. It turned out that Flavigny believed that the 3rd Armoured Division was situated just west of the Ardennes Canal and could be brought across immediately to counter-attack, together with the 3rd Motorized Division, towards the Bois de la Marfée, and that he was expecting the counter-attack to be launched at eleven o'clock. Brocard at once realized that this would be impossible. He did, however, promise to do what he could to see that his division arrived before nightfall.

The armour struggled towards the jumping-off point throughout the whole of the 14th, the tanks and vehicles fighting their way along roads pitted with bomb- and shell-craters and crammed with streams of soldiers fleeing from the front in disorder. The exhausted division began to assemble along a line between Tannay and Stonne in the late afternoon, only to find that the infantry that was to take part in the counter-attack had not arrived. By the time they did, it was too late, and Flavigny was left with no alternative but to cancel the counter-attack. Instead he ordered Brocard and the commander of the 3rd Motorized to split up their forces and place groups of infantry and tanks on the approach roads to the area, and there they remained throughout the early hours of 15 May. Then at 06.15 General Georges, realizing far more plainly than Flavigny or Huntziger the true extent to which the situation was deteriorating, ordered the counter-attack to go ahead and sent instructions to Flavigny to attack northwards with the 3rd Armoured Division in an attempt to reach the Meuse at Wadelincourt. As before, the armour was to be supported by the 3rd Motorized Division. General Roucaud's 1st Colonial Division and the 2nd Cavalry Division were also to attack on the right of XXI Corps. Zero hour was to be 15.00 hours. The Germans, meanwhile, were making rapid progress to meet just such a French move. As the 1st Panzer Division swung right to the River Bar on the 14th, its place was taken by the 10th Panzer and the Grossdeutschland Regiment. On the morning of the 15th, 10th Panzer was strengthened by the arrival of units of the German 29th Motorized Division. At 07.00 the Germans launched a strong attack against the village of Stonne, which held a commanding position on high ground and which was occupied by the 67th Cavalry Regiment of the 3rd Motorized Division. The French force was compelled to withdraw, but a counter-attack was immediately launched by the Hotchkiss tanks of the 45th Battalion and a company of B.1s of the 49th, supported by an infantry battalion of the 67th. Stonne was recaptured after a bitter fight. The French held on to the village determinedly all that day, resisting continual German pressure, but at nightfall the Germans launched another major attack and once again recaptured the objective.

At 15.00 hours, with the French still in occupation of Stonne, the long-awaited French armoured counter-attack at last began to get under way. It was doomed to failure, the French force being drastically depleted thanks to Flavigny's earlier order to divide it. Apart from the fact that there was no sign of the B tanks from the 41st Battalion, which had been attached to the Chanoine Group across the Ardennes Canal, one of the three companies of Colonel Préclaire's 49th Battalion was engaged in the battle for Stonne, which effectively reduced the attacking force to one heavy and one light battalion of tanks and one infantry battalion. Nevertheless the tanks set out, with a company of B.1s moving forward on either side of the Sedan road supported by a few Hotchkiss. There was no artillery support, no liaison with the infantry and – still more serious – no attempt to reconnoitre the ground ahead. Soon after setting out, the tanks ran into a large French anti-tank ditch running along the entire front. There was only one crossing point, and when the tanks tried to get into single file to move over, they presented an unparalleled target for a battery of German 88-mm anti-tank guns which had held their fire until this moment. Within minutes, five of the B tanks were in flames, and the remainder retreated back the way they had come. It was only when they arrived back at their starting line that the tank commanders learned that General Flavigny, at last waking up to the inevitable outcome of the counter-attack, had cancelled it fifteen minutes earlier. The sacrificial lamb for this failure was General Brocard, who was relieved of his command and replaced by General Buisson, the commander of the 3rd Motorized Division.

By nightfall on 14 May, few Second and Ninth Army Units remained intact, although one or two formations still clung to their original positions and had not yet been seriously troubled by the enemy. These included the 61st Infantry Division and the 52nd Demi-Brigade, composed of Indo-Chinese machine-gunners, both of them stationed in the Mézières area. It was not until the early hours of the 15th, following the withdrawal of the 22nd Division on the left flank of the 61st, that the latter came into contact with the enemy. At 04.00 a large body of German infantry crossed the river in rubber boats and although the French put up a determined resistance, causing many casualties, the Germans succeeded in establishing a foothold on the left bank, capturing a number of French machine-gun positions. Nevertheless, the line was still holding when General Billotte's orders came for the Ninth Army to retire. At this time it was not known that the 42nd Demi-Brigade at Monthermé had been overwhelmed and that the tanks of the 8th Panzer Division were moving up rapidly from that direction to take the French forces on the river from the rear.

The order to retire reached the 52nd Demi-Brigade while the latter were still involved in a fierce fight with the Germans. The 2nd Battalion pulled back to Mézières and from there moved westwards, gradually disintegrating as it went. At 04.00 it reached Lepren, where it paused while its commander made up his mind what to do. A couple of miles to the west, the village of Marlemont, where regimental HQ should have been, was in flames, its fires forming a lurid twilight. The 52nd's commander consequently decided to make for the River Aisne, and his tired troops got on the march once more. They got as far as Signy l'Abbaye when they ran into a formation of German armoured cars supported by a force of infantry. Since the French had thrown most of their weapons away, the fight lasted only a few minutes. As the sun rose through the clouds of smoke that rolled over the burning countryside, the men of the 52nd Demi-Brigade's 2nd Battalion marched into captivity. The 1st Battalion, some hours behind, was no more fortunate. Unlike the 2nd, which had at least managed to maintain some semblance of cohesion, the 1st Battalion quickly became split up into small groups of men all struggling westwards, and these were easily mopped up by the advancing Germans on the morning of the 16th.

The 61st Division, meanwhile, had been withdrawing from the River Meuse to new positions on a line between Rocroi and Tremblois, a move involving a difficult ten-mile march through dense forest where there were hardly any roads or tracks. The division was intact once more in its new positions by midday on the 14th, but soon afterwards it was practically swamped by the remnants of the 18th and 22nd Divisions and the 1st Cavalry, retreating from the north, and what was left of the 42nd Demi-Brigade and two battalions of the 248th Infantry Regiment from the murderous fight at Monthermé. These dazed, exhausted troops moved through the 61st Division's emplacements in a steady stream, heading westwards, and despite the efforts of its officers, the 61st Division began to break up and move with the general tide, which was being urged on by the 6th and 8th Panzer Divisions following close behind. The Panzers swept through the mass of men almost contemptuously, as did those of Guderian's 1st and 2nd Panzer Divisions to the south. Groups of Frenchmen who were still armed were surrounded and ordered to pile their weapons, which the tanks then drove over to destroy before racing on.

The impossible task of repairing the gaping hole at the junction of the Second and Ninth Armies fell to General Touchon, the commander of XXIII Corps which at that time was in reserve near Dijon. He was given overall command of whatever troops were left in the gap, the 14th Division which was at Reims on its way to the front, and the 2nd Armoured Division whose position no one knew for certain but which was believed to be moving up in support of the French First Army. In short, Touchon had no idea what troops he really had at his disposal with the exception of six training battalions which had no supporting artillery and which were composed mainly of raw recruits. Nevertheless, he did his best and on the afternoon of 15 May, having set up an HQ at Château-Porcien to the north of the Aisne, he set out to find the commander of XLI Corps who should have been at Rumigny. In fact the HQ of XLI Corps was not where it was supposed to be and Touchon had no alternative but to return to his own head-quarters. On the way back, he narrowly escaped being killed when a German machine-gun opened up on his staff car. It was a disturbing incident, particularly as it happened at a point nearly fifteen miles west of the line that Touchon was supposed to defend. Back at Château-Porcien he met General de Lattre, the commander of the 14th Division, who told him that the only effective force he could muster was a single infantry battalion, the 2nd Battalion of 152nd Infantry Regiment.

It was now clear that XLI Corps had ceased to exist, reduced to a sea of scattered fragments through which the Panzer Divisions were driving relentlessly. Nevertheless, by mid-afternoon on the 15th, Touchon had been able to make a more realistic appraisal of the forces at his disposal. First of all there was the Second Army's X Corps, which had been transferred to Touchon's command and which was now optimistically redesignated the Sixth Army. Other units immediately available or moving up to the combat area included the 1st North African Division, which was coming up from Soissons and would not go into action until the 16th; one battalion of the 14th Division in the line, with another moving up; the 36th Infantry Division, which got into position on the Aisne to the east of Rethel; and the 44th and 87th Divisions, both of which were a long way from the front with no chance of reaching it in time – and time was very definitely on the enemy's side.

By midday on the 15th the road for Guderian's 1st and 2nd Panzer Divisions was wide open despite the heroic efforts of the French Chanoine Group, a battalion of the 152nd Infantry Regiment, the 3rd Spahis and the 53rd Division, all of which had fought tenaciously but which were now to all intents and purposes annihilated. The German tanks were now nosing their way into a twenty-mile stretch of rolling hill country, beyond which lay the broad valleys of the Aisne and Oise. They attacked Chagny in the hills, heroically defended by the 8th Chasseurs and Chanoine's Cavalry, while further to the north the 3rd Spahis under Colonel Marc battled until nightfall against hopeless odds against the onslaughts of the 1st Panzer. By 18.00 the French could fight no more. The soot- and oil-blackened tanks rolled into the ruined streets of Chagny, past the burning buildings and the scattered corpses of the French

defenders. All the French officers were either dead or wounded;
the latter included Colonel Marc, who was taken prisoner. A
handful of French troops managed to get away into the woods
before the collapse.

The Germans had a stiff fight on their hands at Bouvellemont,
where the advance of Guderian's armour was resisted by the
152nd Infantry Regiment assisted by General Touchon's training battalions. The French retreated from the blazing village
during the early hours of the morning, and the tanks raced
after them, bypassing French machine-gun nests which were
still firing at dawn. Further to the north the 53rd Division's
208th Infantry Regiment, the 1st Battalion of the 152nd and
troops from a few other scattered units were being pushed
back relentlessly by the 2nd Panzer Division. By dawn on 16
May, the whole Vence Valley had been occupied by the
Germans and what was left of Touchon's forces were falling
back south-westwards towards the River Aisne.

Touchon's last hope, the 2nd Armoured Division under General Bruché, never even got into action. Because of the general
confusion and the delays in providing the necessary heavy
railway tank transporters, the division's heavy tanks did not
leave their loading sites near Revigny until the morning of 14
May, more than twelve hours late. The division's wheeled
echelon of about twelve hundred vehicles had already set off
for the assembly-point at Charleroi, but en route its commander received word that he was heading straight towards
the tanks of Guderian's xIx Panzer Corps, and he decided to
turn the column aside from the congested road and shelter
south of the Aisne. Meanwhile, the division's railway-borne
tanks were de-training at various points, the two Hotchkiss
Battalions at Etreux on the Sambre-Oise Canal a few miles
north of Guise, the 15th Battalion of B.1 tanks at Le Nouvion
and the 8th Battalion of B.1s at Hirson, fifteen miles south-east
of Le Nouvion. More tanks which had not been able to find
transporters were on their way to Charleroi by road. The tanks
that did arrive were split up between Touchon's Sixth Army
and the Ninth Army, and Bruché and his staff spent the next

twenty-four hours driving round the countryside trying to find
out where all the battalions were.

On 18 May, Bruché was in Cambrai when the town was
surrounded by Rommel's 7th Panzer Division. The General and
his staff hid in a stable and succeeded in making their escape
at dawn by mingling with a large column of refugees. On 21
May they finally reached armoured HQ at Compiègne. In the
hours that followed, the 2nd Armoured Division was completely disrupted. One of its columns was attacked near
Cambrai by a Luftwaffe anti-tank unit, II/LG2, flying Henschel
123 biplanes, which knocked out five of the French AFVs while
Messerschmitts strafed the supporting infantry. The remaining
tanks were picked off piecemeal by the armour of the XIV and
XIX Panzer Corps as the latter advanced along the Oise and by
the 88-mm guns of Flak Regiment 33, two batteries of which
were positioned on the approach to Cambrai. The division's
personnel either joined in the general retreat or fought where
they could alongside infantry units that chose to resist the
German advance.

By noon on the 15th, Ninth Army had ceased to exist as an
effective fighting force. During the afternoon General Corap
was relieved of his command and was replaced by General
Giraud, who took over the post with no real idea of the plight
of the forces under his command. He believed, for example,
that the 2nd Armoured Division was immediately at his disposal and ready to go into action, and that other units which
had been decimated and no longer existed except on paper
were still effective. It was not until mid-afternoon that the full
horror of the situation began to make its impact upon him.
He immediately ordered General Bouffet's II Corps, which had
been making an heroic attempt to hold the line on the Meuse
since the previous day, to withdraw to new positions between
Fosse and Mettet and remain there until further orders. The
disengagement of II Corps was carried out without serious
interference from the enemy, except, that is, from the
Luftwaffe. On the morning of the 16th, General Bouffet's
HQ at Bultia was attacked by German dive-bombers, and the

D*

General and several leading members of his staff were killed.

Bouffet's place was taken by General Buché, who had been commanding the 5th Motorized Division and a number of other attached units. By the morning of 17 May the 5th Division – which only a few days earlier had had a total personnel strength of six thousand – had been reduced to four officers and less than a thousand other ranks. Its only remaining weapons were rifles and machine-guns, and there was precious little ammunition. Under the command of Colonel Marioge, what was left of the division was ordered to pull back to Avesnes. The division, however, became badly scattered *en route* and was eventually overrun by the Panzers. Its last surviving unit, a battalion of the 39th Infantry Regiment which had been in Army Reserve, was overwhelmed by Rommel's 7th Panzer near Avesnes on the 18th.

Despite the overall chaos, some Ninth Army unit commanders made gallant attempts to rally their men and resist the invaders. In the Saint Michel forest, for example, General Béziers de la Fosse, the commander of the dislocated 22nd Infantry Division, formed a scratch defence with groups of stragglers of the 62nd and 116th Regiments of the 22nd Division, the 125th of the 18th Division and groups of soldiers from the 4th North African and 5th Moroccan divisions which had got separated from their main force. These men occupied a line of unfinished pill boxes and earthworks in the forest and were prepared to go down fighting. In the event, they surrendered only when they ran out of ammunition.

Rommel, meanwhile, on the orders of General von Kluge, commander of the Fourth Army, was exploiting his successes by launching an attack on the morning of the 16th against remaining French defences between the River Sambre and the forest of Saint Michel. Much of this defensive line was unfinished and was garrisoned by only six battalions of 101st Division. Rommel launched his attack with one armoured battalion at the line's weakest point, between Clairfayts and the Sambre, which was garrisoned by the 84th Fortress Infantry

Regiment. His tanks moved through Sivry just inside Belgian territory, which was deserted, and halted short of Clairfayts while the Luftwaffe subjected it to an intense air attack. By eight o'clock the defenders, a single company of the 84th, were unable to resist any longer. An artillery barrage finished them off, and under cover of heavy machine-gun fire, Rommel's engineers moved forward to clear obstacles in their path.

Rommel's tanks thundered on. Sweeping aside isolated pockets of resistance, they raced through the village of Solre-le-Château, capturing five batteries of 75-mm guns belonging to the 1st Armoured Division before the French gunners had a chance to fire a shot. At 02.00 on the 17th, Rommel's tanks were storming Avesnes from the west, wiping out seventeen tanks of the 25th Hotchkiss Battalion in one whirlwind engagement. Ignoring groups of bewildered French troops who looked on helplessly, they plunged on to occupy a crossing on the Sambre at Landrecies, ten miles away, the speeding armour thrusting aside columns of refugees and soldiers that crowded the road. By 06.00 Rommel's leading tanks were in sight of le Câteau. Their exhausted crews emerged from the stifling, reeking interiors of the armoured monsters and thankfully gulped in lungfuls of fresh morning air. They had advanced fifty miles in less than eighteen hours, almost non-stop.

Although Rommel's audacious dash to the Sambre had paid dividends, he was all too conscious of the risks he still ran. His tank battalion was almost out of fuel and ammunition, and it would be some time before the remainder of the Panzer Division arrived. Moreover, in his rear there were considerable numbers of French troops who still retained their arms and who had not yet surrendered. Fortunately the French seemed unaware that Rommel had progressed so far, but as a security precaution he withdrew to Avesnes in the course of the morning.

For the Ninth Army, there was no longer any pretence of cohesive resistance. At 04.00 on the 17th, General Giraud ordered the remnants of his command to the Sambre-Oise Canal. In the north, General Blanchard's First Army – its right

flank now exposed by the withdrawal of the Ninth – was also
pulling out of Belgium, its men trudging along the dusty
Belgian roads west of Liège under continual air attack. Further
north still, the British Expeditionary Force and the remaining
Belgian divisions were embarking on a fighting retreat, remaining only long enough to cover the First Army while its right
flank fell back to Charleroi. Only a week after the start of the
German attack, the allied defensive plan was in a state of total
collapse, yet General Giraud still appeared blind to the fact
that everything was lost. He continued to organize his divisions as though the shattered remnants of his force were still
fully equipped combat units, moving his HQ to le Câtelet and
making plans for counter-attacks with forces that no longer
existed.

General Giraud's staff reached le Câtelet before the General
himself, a fact that probably saved his life. As he was approaching the town, it came under heavy fire from leading elements
of the 8th Panzer Division. The Ninth Army HQ was wiped out
and many senior officers were killed or wounded. Giraud
turned back the way he had come, emptied the contents of his
briefcase into a ditch and set fire to them. Some time later, he
was picked up by a unit of the 2nd Armoured Division. That
was on the 18th. The following morning, the General and his
companions were captured by German troops.

For the Ninth Army, it was the end. Like the tentacles of
some great armoured octopus, the columns of the seven Panzer
divisions were relentlessly extending their grasp on Belgium
and Northern France. They had mopped up the Ardennes
forest, thrown themselves over the Meuse and were now slicing
with near incredible speed through the shattered remnants
of France's broken armies. In the south, the 1st Panzer of
Guderian's XIX Armoured Corps, flanked by the 2nd Panzer
on its right and the 10th on its left, was approaching the Oise
in two groups, one north of Saint Quentin, the other to the
south. In the centre, the 6th and 8th Divisions of Reinhardt's
XLI Corps were also approaching the Oise by way of Rubigny
and Vervins. These spearheads were followed up by the three

divisions of the 14th Motorized Corps. In the north were the
5th and 7th Armoured Divisions of General Hoth's Armoured
Group, with the task of outflanking the northern allied armies
by cutting through to the line extending from Maubeuge
through Cambrai to Arras. Coming hard up behind Hoth's
forces were the 3rd and 4th Panzer Divisions and the 20th
Motorized Division of xvi Armoured Corps, which had been
diverted from von Bock's Army Group b.

The rapid German advance, however, was causing considerable concern at German Army High Command hq, where
Hitler expressed the view that the rapid thrust was leaving the
southern flank of the German front dangerously open to a
French counter-attack. Protecting the invasion's left flank in
fact soon became an obsession, and when Hitler visited Army
Group hq at Charleville on the morning of the 17th, he warned
von Rundstedt that everything was to be done to secure the
flank. He also ordered von Kleist's armour not to proceed beyond the Oise until further orders, while General List's Twelfth
Army was to swing south-westwards and take up defensive
positions. The consequences of these orders were described by
General Guderian :

Early on 17 May I received a message from the Panzer Group :
the advance was to be halted at once and I was personally to report
to General von Kleist, who would come to see me at my airstrip
at 07.00 hours. He was there punctually and, without even wishing
me a good morning, began in very violent terms to berate me for
having disobeyed orders. He did not see fit to waste a word of
praise on the performance of the troops. When the first storm was
passed, and he had stopped to draw breath, I asked that I might be
relieved of my command. General von Kleist was momentarily
taken aback, but then he nodded and ordered me to hand over my
command to the most senior general of my corps. And that was
the end of our conversation. I returned to my corps headquarters
and asked General Veiel to come to see me, that I might hand over
to him.

I then sent a message to Army Group von Rundstedt by wireless
in which I said that after I had handed over my command at noon,
I would be flying to the Army Group headquarters to make a

report on what had happened. I received an answer almost at once: I was to remain at my headquarters and await the arrival of Colonel-General List, who was in command of the Twelfth Army that was following behind us and who had been instructed to clear this matter up. Until the arrival of Colonel-General List, all units were to be ordered to remain where they were. Major Wenck, who came to receive these orders, was shot at by a French tank while returning to his division and was wounded in the foot. General Veiel now appeared and I explained the situation to him. Early that afternoon Colonel-General List arrived and asked me at once what on earth was going on here. Acting on instructions from Colonel-General von Rundstedt, he informed me that I would not resign my command and explained that the order to halt the advance came from the Army High Command (the OKH) and there- fore must be obeyed. He quite understood my reasons, however, for wishing to go on with the advance and therefore, with the Army Group's approval, he ordered: 'Reconnaissance in force to be carried out. Corps headquarters must in all circumstances re- main where it is, so that it may be easily reached.' This was at least something, and I was grateful to Colonel-General List for what he had done. I asked him to clear up the misunderstanding between General von Kleist and myself. Then I set the 'reconnais- sance in force' in motion.

The general concern for the security of the German southern flank and the emphasis on the rapid thrust in the centre all tended to slow down the impetus of German operations north of the River Sambre where, between Antwerp and Namur, fifteen under-armed Belgian divisions, eight British and nine French, and three light armoured divisions, confronted fifteen German divisions in the line and six in reserve, a force that could be reinforced rapidly with another army if the situation demanded it. The German High Command in fact regarded this area of operations as being of minor importance, and it was for this reason that on the 16th General Hoeppner's XVI Panzer Corps was diverted from von Bock's command to reinforce von Rundstedt's army group to the south of Namur.

On the 17th the Germans crossed the River Sambre and were openly approaching Maubeuge and the Forest of Mormal, where the defence line was held by the 4th Demi-Brigade of Chasseurs à Pied, the 3rd Moroccans, the 101st Fortress Division and 158th Cavalry Regiment of the 43rd Division. Towards the evening of the 17th, advance units of the 4th Infantry Division also began to arrive at Denain and Valenciennes, having carried out a forced march from Belgium on the orders of General Billotte. By this time the Germans had penetrated the Forest of Mormal, and Billotte instructed the First Army to drive them out. This operation was to be carried out by the 5th North Africans, supported by two battalions of the 3rd Moroccans and a battalion of tanks from the 2nd Light Armoured Division.

The attack, under the command of General Mesny, was launched just before dusk on the 19th, the whole operation having been delayed for twenty-four hours because of the difficulty of moving troops and equipment up to the jump-off point under constant air attack. In the small hours the attacking force reached the first objective, the railway line running between Berlaimont and Le Quesnoy, but the Germans rapidly reinforced their troops and succeeded in surrounding the French right flank near Englefontaine. By this time the French armoured support had fallen apart through lack of fuel, and it was only with the greatest difficulty that General Mesny managed to extricate most of his forces from the rapidly closing trap. In fact, it would probably not have been possible at all had it not been for the proficiency of the French artillery, whose 75-mms knocked out several German tanks, enabling most of the French column to pass through the line of the River Escaut on the evening of the 21st.

The 43rd Division, meanwhile, had abandoned most of its positions, and its troops were beginning the long march westwards. This move, however, was forestalled by a heavy German attack on the French fortified positions at Bavai, and the remaining seven battalions of the 43rd found themselves involved in fierce fighting. One by one they were annihilated, except for a few men who managed to get away. This battle saw one of the most gallant actions of the whole campaign when the 10th Chasseurs battalion, forming the rearguard, was trapped and assailed by a whole German infantry regiment. The Chasseurs fought on until their ammunition was exhausted, then they burned their colours, fixed bayonets and charged the enemy. They were mown down to a man by the German machine-guns.

The battle in the vicinity of the Forest of Mormal marked the virtual end of the First Army v Corps. Only one division, the 12th, managed to withdraw successfully with few casualties, to rejoin the First Army HQ after passing through Valenciennes. The division was subsequently attached to III Corps which, together with IV Corps, had managed to withdraw behind the line of the River Escaut. As they withdrew, these formations were joined by scattered fragments of Ninth Army units which had managed to stay ahead of the advance of Reinhardt's XLI Panzer Corps. All were falling back towards the Escaut where a line was building up along the river to Bouchain, then north of the Senseé as far as the Canal du Nord and on to the Scarpe, which was lined by a British infantry brigade as far as Arras.

As late as the morning of 17 May, it was still believed at the French GHQ that the right flank of the Ninth Army was still in contact with the left flank of the Sixth, and that, although this junction was extremely fragile and under constant pressure, it should be possible to weld it with the introduction of a new army. The task of forming this new army was given to General Frère, who had been commanding VIII Corps in Lorraine. Five divisions, practically the last of the French Army's reserves, went into its make-up. With orders to deny passage through the Oise Valley to the Germans and link up with the right of the Ninth Army near Ribemont, Frère set up his HQ at Roye and ordered the two divisions immediately available to him to occupy the line of the Somme River from Ham to the Crozat Canal and the canal itself as far as the Oise. Even at this stage, the staff of the French Army HQ North East were still thinking in terms of launching a strong armoured counter-attack against the invading German forces. They were not yet aware that the only armoured formation at their disposal was the embryo 4th Division under the command of Colonel Charles de Gaulle, which lay in the open country between the forward elements of General Guderian's 1st Panzer Division and the River Oise.

De Gaulle established a mobile HQ at Bruyères on 15 May, where he was joined the following day by the 6th Armoured Brigade consisting of two companies of B tanks and one of D2s, a total of thirty-five vehicles. A few hours later the 8th Brigade also arrived. This comprised the 24th Battalion and a company of the 2nd with a total of fifty Renault tanks. On the 17th the formation's ranks were swelled by the 322nd Artillery Regiment with 105-mm guns and the 4th Chasseurs. It was an entirely makeshift force and totally inadequate for the task it was supposed to perform. There was a shortage of ammunition, no signalling equipment or radio of any kind, most of the personnel were only partly trained and the crews of de Gaulle's B tanks had come straight off the lighter Hotchkiss vehicles and had no experience of the heavier armour.

The first objective for de Gaulle's two scratch armoured brigades was the village of Montcornet, which had recently been captured by Guderian and commanded a strategic position on the crossroads leading to Saint Quentin, Laon and Reims. The 6th Brigade approached the objective from Laon, following the left flank of the road, while on the right the 8th Brigade passed through Boncourt and Ville aux Bois, each column being followed up by a detachment of the 2nd Dismounted Dragoons and some groups of Chasseurs. On the way the tanks of the left-hand column had to pass over a causeway across some marshes near Liesse. At the other side they ran into a small group of German tanks, and there was a confused skirmish in which one or two soft-skinned vehicles were destroyed. This fight occurred before all the B tanks had got across the marshes successfully; six of them slid off the road and became hopelessly bogged down.

The attack against Montcornet was launched in daylight and de Gaulle's tanks penetrated into the outskirts of the village. With only one battalion of Chasseurs to support them, however, they could not hold on and were compelled to withdraw after knocking out a single German tank. De Gaulle's forces were withdrawn during the late afternoon, attacked by German aircraft all the way, and found shelter in the forest of Samoussy between Sissonne and Bruyères. The absence of any French air support and effective artillery contributed to making the 4th Division's position quite untenable. As de Gaulle himself commented: 'We were lost children thirty kilometres in front of the Aisne and we had to end a situation which was hazardous, to say the least.'

The next day, however, the situation brightened a little with the arrival of the 7th Motorized Dragoon Regiment, two squadrons of armoured cars of the 10th Cuirassiers and a group of the 3rd Cuirassiers armed with forty of the excellent Somua cavalry tanks. The new arrivals came just in time, for by the morning of the 18th the 4th Division had only twenty B and forty Renault tanks left. On the 19th, with the aid of these reinforcements, de Gaulle was ordered by General Touchon to cross the River Serre and attack Guderian's lines of communication. The attack was launched at 07.00, the French tanks moving forward in three parallel columns, but by this time the Germans had had ample time to mine the approaches to the Serre bridges and bring up their anti-tank batteries, and before the attack had been under way half an hour, the Stukas appeared in full strength. By 09.00 de Gaulle's thrust had ground to a halt, while on its right flank the supporting infantry were attacked again and again by bombers and by the tanks of 10th Panzer and the mechanized infantry of the 29th Motorized Division.

Desperate though the French situation was, General Touchon asked de Gaulle to hold on for twenty-four hours until the 28th Infantry had time to establish a defensive line on the Ailette River. The 4th Armoured's infantry therefore clung to their positions just short of Laon and suffered further enemy attacks throughout the night, finally extricating themselves with great difficulty the following morning. The gallant failure of de Gaulle's small counter-offensive marked the French Army's last chance to redress the balance at this crucial stage of the battle with the aid of armour. At nightfall on the 20th, what was left of the division pulled back over the Aisne and concentrated around Fismes. There was no doubt that its unexpected resistance had shaken the Germans, but it had never represented a serious threat and it had accomplished nothing. Nevertheless, if the commanders of the other French armoured divisions had conducted their operations with the same dash as de Gaulle, the story of May 1940 might have been a very different one.

Meanwhile, on the 18th, General Frère was still making determined efforts to establish a defensive line along the Somme and the Crozat Canal with the meagre forces at his disposal, consisting mainly of the advance parties of his two divisions, the 3rd Light and the 23rd. The Germans, however, succeeded in bypassing the Crozat Canal by slipping across the Oise between Moy and Landrecies, brushing aside the tanks of the 2nd Armoured Division and driving on to Péronne. They succeeded in pushing bridges across the river at the latter town, but at Ham they came into contact with Frère's 23rd Division and were thrown back. On the 19th, however, Péronne was taken, and the German armour began to cross the Somme in great strength. On the 20th the 1st Panzer Division captured a British battalion at Albert and then drove on to attack Amiens, which had been subjected to heavy Luftwaffe raids and which was in flames from end to end. There it threw back two battalions of the Royal Sussex Regiment and a French Territorial unit and occupied the plateau to the south of the city.

Simultaneously, the 2nd Panzer Division raced on to Abbeville where for the first time, the tank crews got sight of the English Channel. The Panzers cut through the British 35th Brigade and dislocated it, pushing patrols for another twenty miles down the coast and capturing the vital river crossing at St Valéry-sur-Somme. Apart from a brush between the 1st Panzer and reconnaissance group of the French 1 Corps, coming down from Belgian territory at Corbie on the Somme, neither of the Panzer divisions met serious opposition. The overwhelming Luftwaffe air superiority and the almost total lack of allied countermeasures were having a telling effect on the outcome of the battle.

On the morning of the 21st, the 1st and 2nd Panzer Divisions were relieved by Guderian's 10th Panzer at Amiens, Picquigny, Abbeville and St Valéry-sur-Somme, and after a short rest, the 1st and 2nd Panzer began to push northwards along the coast with the objective of widening the rift between the allied armies to the north and south.

CHAPTER 5

The British Expeditionary Force: The Road to Dunkirk

While the Wehrmacht smashed its way through the Meuse defences to the south, the British Expeditionary Force in the north became hemmed in between the Belgian and the First French Armies and made little serious contact with the enemy forces during the first few days. In accordance with General Gamelin's orders, the first reconnaissance units of the British Expeditionary Force had reached the River Dyle on the night of 10 May, and in the days that followed, the Dyle line was manned between Louvain and Wavre along a seventeen-mile front by the 1st, 2nd and 3rd Divisions of I and II Corps, with the 4th and 48th Divisions in reserve positions. Further to the rear, the 42nd and 46th Infantry Divisions worked desperately to prepare defensive positions along the Escaut Line while the 5th and 50th Divisions formed GHQ reserve.

It was not until the afternoon of 14 May that all elements of I and II Corps were in position on the Dyle in readiness to meet the expected German attack. On the 15th the Germans launched an assault against the 3rd Division in the Louvain area but failed to gain much ground. That night, however, they launched a heavy artillery attack on the 2nd Division's area at Wavre and soon afterwards the division was compelled to pull out of the line to conform with the withdrawal of the French First Army on the right flank, the units pulling back towards the Senne river. Meanwhile, another BEF division, the 5th, which had been concentrated around Amiens when the Germans attacked on the 10th, embarked on a series of forced marches towards the River Senne to support the other units already there. Some of the divisional units had motor transport at their disposal, but in other cases the men were forced to proceed on foot, an exhausting business in the hot May weather. The 2nd Northamptons of 17th Infantry Brigade, for example, marched twenty-five miles from Camps-en-Amiennois to Bernaville on the 11th followed by twelve miles at Ligny-sur-Cache on the 12th and a further thirteen miles to Hernicourt on the 15th, finally arriving in the Hal area on the afternoon of the 16th. During the latter stages of the journey, the battalion had been forced to fight its way through masses of Belgian refugees which clogged all the roads.

The 13th Infantry Brigade dug itself in around Hal, close to the old battlefield of Waterloo, with the 2nd Battalion Royal Inniskilling Fusiliers providing the garrison for the town itself. The 17th Infantry Brigade dug in some distance to the north. The remainder of the Senne line was occupied by the 4th Infantry Division. On the 16th, as the First French Army withdrew to the south, General Billotte issued orders for the BEF to withdraw to the Escaut Line. The divisions manning the Dyle line were pulled out that same night, and along the River Senne the 4th and 5th Divisions prepared to make contact with the enemy who would not be far in their wake. At the same time, General Giraud's Seventh Army – following its rapid movement up the coast of Belgium and Holland – withdrew around the rear of the BEF, leaving the Belgian Army fighting on the Expeditionary Force's left flank. The 48th Division now withdrew through the lines of the 5th Division, which had been dug in since 10.00 hours on the 17th with the 1st Division on its left.

As yet, the divisions manning the Senne line had made no contact with the enemy, with the exception of a few German observation aircraft which flew overhead at a respectable altitude and were fired on without much success by the light anti-aircraft machine-gun platoons of the 2nd Division. The first serious air attack came on the afternoon of the 17th, when the 5th Division HQ was dive-bombed by Stukas. The division's anti-aircraft machine-gunners claimed to have hit one of the enemy aircraft. The 5th Division's first encounter with German ground forces occurred near Hal, when a group of German cyclists were sighted across the canal by the 2nd Royal Inniskillings. A small detachment under Major Butler went over to engage them, and the Germans retreated after losing three dead and two wounded. That evening, the Germans attacked in strength but they were unable to penetrate the British line thanks to some highly accurate supporting fire by the artillery of 1 Corps, which kept up a continuous barrage on the attackers from prepared positions behind the Senne. However, the French forces on the southern flank of the BEF were being steadily pushed back, and before long the British divisions were compelled to withdraw to maintain the line.

The troops fell back towards the River Dendre, which was the next line of defence before the main positions on the Escaut Line. The withdrawal was attended by a certain amount of confusion, which was not alleviated by the fact that there was a serious shortage of maps. To make matters worse, the British were under considerable pressure from the attacking Germans, and some units had considerable difficulty in disengaging. This was particularly true of the 13th Infantry Brigade where two companies of the 2nd Royal Inniskillings in Hal missed the flank line and had to find their way across country to join the battalion as it crossed the River Dendre two days later. During daylight hours the withdrawal was harassed by continual enemy air attack, and there were the usual streams of refugees to impede progress. Some units only just managed to get across the bridges on the River Dendre before they were blown.

While this withdrawal was in progress, von Kleist's Panzers received orders to renew their offensive and advance to Cambrai and St Quentin, a move which placed the right – or southern – flank of the BEF in danger. Although there was an overall lack of firm intelligence, Lord Gort, the BEF's commander, took immediate steps to strengthen the garrison at Arras which lay in the path of the German tanks. Within twenty-four hours, the town's garrison, at that time comprising the 1st Welsh Guards, had been bolstered by a scratch force of troops drawn from miscellaneous units together with three territorial divisions, the 12th, 23rd and 46th, all of them training divisions on lines of communication duties. This enlarged force was put under the command of Major General R. L. Petre and became known as Petreforce.

By 18 May it was clear that unless the rift between the allied armies caused by the German armoured spearheads could be closed, the British Expeditionary Force would be compelled to retreat to the line of the River Somme or evacuate from the Channel ports. With the progress the Germans were making, even the possibility of withdrawing to the Somme became more remote with every passing hour. Meanwhile, the BEF divisions in the line were involved in heavy fighting as they withdrew to the Escaut Line on that same day. Of the two divisions in reserve, the 5th was assembling around Seclin and the 50th was moving back from Athies on the Dendre River – where it had been involved in three days of fierce fighting – to the Vimy Ridge area. On the 19th the reconnaissance groups of Rommel's 7th Panzer, or, to be more precise, Rothenburg's 25th Panzer Regiment, came into contact with the British defences at Arras. The German tanks halted, being badly over-extended with their supporting infantry a long way behind.

At this juncture, Lord Gort evolved a daring plan designed to strike hard at the flank of the German armoured advance. The following day he sent for Major General H. E. Franklyn, commanding the 5th Division, and informed him that he wished the 5th to operate in and around Arras with a three-fold mission that included, first, dealing with any enemy that might be encountered en route; second, relieving French armoured troops holding the line of the River Scarpe to the east of Arras and also any British troops still in position there; and third, making Arras secure with the object of gaining as much elbow room as possible south of the town. Franklyn later recalled that Gort's manner was imperturbable and that he frequently used the expression 'mopping up'. 'I am still unable to understand', Franklyn wrote, 'why he painted such a distorted picture. At the time there were seven German armoured divisions operating between Arras and the River Somme twenty miles further south, rather a tall order for me to mop up.'

As well as his own 5th Division, Franklyn was also assigned the 50th under General Martel to carry out the task, together with the 1st Army Tank Brigade under Brigadier Douglas Pratt. This, the one and only tank brigade in the BEF, had suffered badly from mechanical trouble. Its two battalions, the 4th and 7th Royal Tank Regiment, had fifty-eight machine-gun-armed Mk I Matilda tanks, but only sixteen of the later Mk IIs armed with 2-pounder guns. These tanks, although heavily armoured, were slower than the German Mk IVs, but could match them in most other respects. After receiving his orders, Franklyn went to Vimy, about ten miles north of Arras, to meet General Martel, who had already ordered his leading brigade – including the 4th and 5th Green Howards – to move forward to Arras and hold the line of the River Scarpe east of the town. After consultation with Martel, Franklyn immediately arranged for the 5th Division's leading brigade to relieve the 23rd Infantry Division and the French Cavalry who were positioned on the Scarpe.

Franklyn and Martel then went to see General Prioux, commanding the French Armoured Corps, some of whose forces were to be relieved by the BEF. Franklyn found the French General pleasant, cheerful and obviously efficient. General Altmayer, commanding the French V Corps, was also present. It was this Corps that the 13th Brigade were to get in touch with. Altmayer presented a complete contrast to the effervescent Prioux. He was haggard and worried looking, poring over a map covered with many coloured lines.

Standing behind Altmayer [Franklyn recalled] was a small, wizened man who was quite unknown to me. I shook hands with him but only long afterwards did I find out that he was General Billotte, the Supreme Commander to the north of the 'Gap'. Actually, neither Martel nor I had ever heard of him: we had been busily engaged during the previous ten days on a much lower level. Billotte was in a hurry to leave and we had no conversation, but what a missed opportunity! Here was the commander of the French and British armies, who, by a stroke of luck, found assembled in one room all the commanders who would be mainly responsible for any attack southwards. If only he had taken me into his confidence, I would have rung up Gort and got confirmation that I was to take part in an attack southwards in conjunction with the French; an operation which alone stood even the faint chance of averting the disaster looming ahead. After Billotte had left, Altmayer spread out the map and told me that he was proposing to attack southwards on the next day and asked me if I was ready to join in. I got the impression that this was his own idea and that he was only half-hearted about it. I cannot imagine why neither he nor Prioux explained that the orders for this attack had been just delivered in person by the Commander-in-Chief. Maybe I should have put two and two together, but neither Martel nor I did so. An attack on the scale proposed seemed quite beyond the instructions which I had received from Gort and, when I explained this, Altmayer seemed relieved. It was clear that he had very little faith in the project.

Together with Martel, Franklyn thrashed out the operational plan. Of the forces at his disposal, the 13th Infantry Brigade was in the process of relieving the Franco-British forces on the Scarpe, the 17th Infantry Brigade was to be held in reserve on Vimy Ridge until the first phase of the advance around Arras – to be made by the 151st Infantry Brigade of 50th Division – was completed, while the other brigade, the 150th, was sent to strengthen Arras and that part of the Scarpe that lay between it and the 13th Infantry Brigade. The plan called for the 151st Infantry Brigade to sweep around Arras to the Cojeul River, while in the second phase the 13th Infantry Brigade was to advance over the Scarpe and join up with the 151st Infantry Brigade to the south of Arras, the infantry working in close co-operation with the Army Tank Brigade.

The whole plan, in fact, was devised to give the tanks the fullest possible scope. It would have been difficult to move them east of Arras, for at this point the River Scarpe was a serious obstacle whereas west of the town it was not. It was also inadvisable to move the tanks through Arras itself, for after moving through the narrow streets, which in all probability were blocked with rubble, it would be well-nigh impossible for the armour to emerge on the other side of the town with any semblance of order. The attack would therefore have to proceed west of the town, swinging around it at fairly close range in a tight semi-circle in order to protect its left flank. The attack was to be supported by six regiments of artillery. Franklyn also asked for air support but the depleted state of the AASF and the BEF's air component made this impossible. As an added safeguard, General Prioux agreed to manœuvre the armour at his disposal to protect the exposed right flank of the attack.

I now made my first great mistake [Franklyn later admitted]. The attack around Arras had gradually become so much bigger than was originally envisaged that now it was of a scope sufficiently great to co-operate with General Altmayer's attack southwards, which he had proposed to me. It is perhaps doubtful if he could have mounted a Corps attack in the time available, but I should have given him the chance to do so. Many months later, when the first accounts of this campaign were published, together with Gort's despatches, I was horrified to find that Altmayer was accused of letting me down. After the surrender of France in June, Altmayer, who must have heard of this untruth, got a message through to me: 'Tell General Franklyn', he said, 'that I did not let him down'.

At 06.00 on 21 May, General Franklyn called together his subordinate commanders to give them their final briefing. The operation in the field was to be commanded by the newly-promoted Major-General Martel. Apart from the fact that he was commander of one of the divisions involved, his enthusiasm for armoured warfare during the thirties was legendary throughout the British Army, which made him eminently suitable to lead a joint armour/infantry operation of this kind. His plan was to form the tank/infantry force into the two columns, each containing a field and anti-tank battery and each commanded by an infantryman. H hour was fixed for 11.00, but on Martel's insistence – there was some delay in assembling the force – this was postponed until 14.00. It would take every one of the intervening hours to tie up the necessary plans for co-ordination between the tanks and infantry.

Meanwhile, in the rear, at Allied High Command, the whole situation was rapidly getting out of control. General Billotte had been killed in a motor accident and for some time the allied commanders, including Lord Gort, were left with no one to give them orders. It was almost impossible for unit commanders to co-ordinate their plans, for the Luftwaffe had shattered telephone communications, and it was equally as difficult to get from place to place on the congested roads. One example of this breakdown in communications was spotlighted when General Weygand called a conference after he had been appointed Supreme Commander of both French and British Armies. The message took so long to reach Lord Gort that by the time he reached Ypres, where the conference was to be held, it was to find that everything was over and that Weygand had left.

Nevertheless, both Franklyn and Martel were fairly optimistic about the chances of the coming operation. The attack began on schedule at 14.00, and although resistance was met much earlier than had been expected, since the Germans had been pushing forward during the morning, the British armour made good progress. It was the first counterstroke that the Germans had met in their triumphant dash to the sea, and it came as an unpleasant surprise to them. Rommel's 7th Panzer Division was at this moment in the process of advancing around Arras towards the north-west, with the ss Totenkopf Motorized Division on his left and the 5th Panzer Division on his right. He later wrote:

I had actually intended to accompany the tanks myself together with Lieutenant Most (Rommel's ADC), my despatch riders, armoured car and signals vehicle, and to conduct operations from there by wireless, but the infantry regiments were so slow in backing up that I drove straight off back to chase up the 7th Rifle Regiment and get it to hurry. It was nowhere to be found. A mile or so north of Ficheux we eventually came across part of the 6th Rifle Regiment, and driving alongside their column, turned off with 'them towards Wailly. Half a mile east of the village we came under fire from the north.

Although Rommel did not know it at the time, he had passed right across both of Martel's tank columns, which now fell on the astonished infantry of the 7th Division, the Rifle Regiments and the supporting troops of the Totenkopf Division. With no hope of support from their own armour – the German tanks had raced on so far ahead that they would not be able to return to the scene of the battle for some time – the sudden onslaught by the British Matildas threw the German infantry into total confusion. In Rommel's words:

The enemy tank fire had created chaos among our troops, and they were jamming up the roads and yards with their vehicles instead of going into action with every available weapon to fight off the enemy. We tried to create order. The crew of a howitzer battery, some distance away, now left their guns, swept along by the retreating infantry. With Most's help, I brought every available gun into action against the tanks. Every gun, both anti-tank and anti-aircraft, was ordered to open rapid fire immediately and I personally gave each gun its target. When the enemy tanks came perilously close, only rapid fire from every gun could save the situation.

The German anti-tank gunners were horrified to find that their shells simply bounced off the Matildas' heavy armour, and when the infantry saw that their anti-tank guns were useless, those that were not killed or captured began to run, throwing away their weapons. The ss Totenkopf Division in particular, as General Guderian later recalled, showed signs of panic. After the battle, the British Tank Brigade Commander, Pratt, told how the Matildas

played hell with a lot of Boche motor transport and their kindred stuff. Tracer ammunition put a lot up in flames. His anti-tank gunners, after firing a bit, bolted and left their guns, even when fired on at ranges of six to eight hundred yards from Matildas.

Some surrendered and others feigned dead on the ground. None of his anti-tank stuff penetrated our is and iis, and not even did his field artillery which fired high explosive. Some tracks were broken, and a few tanks were put on fire by his tracer bullets, chiefly in the engine compartment of the Matilda is. One Matilda had fourteen direct hits from his 37-mm guns, and it had no harmful effect, just gouged out a bit of armour. The main opposition came from his field guns, some of which fired over open sights. Also the air dive-bombing on the infantry – this, of course, did not worry the tanks much. One or two bombs bursting alongside a Matilda turned it over and killed the commander; another lifted a light tank about fifteen feet in the air. Had we only been able to stage a methodical battle with a series of reasonably short objectives, with some artillery support and even a little air support and no frantic rush, we should have done far better and saved many lives of fellows we cannot afford to lose.

In fact the British thrust came to a halt when it came up against the 88-mm anti-aircraft guns, hastily turned into anti-tank weapons on Rommel's orders and firing over open sights. Not even the Matildas' weight of armour could withstand their high velocity shells, and the attack eventually ground to a halt just as it was about to complete the semi-circle around Arras. The British casualty list was fairly heavy, but the losses of the 7th Panzer Division were heavier still. According to the Germans, they numbered 89 killed, 116 wounded, and 173 missing. Added to this the British took 400 prisoners, most of them from the Totenkopf Division, and on this one day alone, Rommel's division suffered four times the losses it had sustained during the breakthrough across the Meuse. The attack had achieved such complete surprise that at one stage Rommel thought he was being confronted by no fewer than five divisions, and later recorded that the battle had been fought against hundreds of enemy tanks.

During the advance, the 13th Infantry Brigade managed to secure a bridgehead over the Scarpe in preparation for the second part of the British advance. It was destined never to take place. Although the British attack gave the Germans a bloody nose and worried them sufficiently to make them hesitate in their forward drive, the BEF was not sufficiently strong to exploit its initial advantage by breaking through the Germans completely and presenting a serious threat to their lines of communication. That night the Luftwaffe intervened, with dive-bombers making a series of heavy attacks on the villages held by the British infantry. The troops could only weather the storm as best they could, shaking their fists impotently at the dive-bombers, loosing off an occasional burst of small arms fire at them and cursing at the lack of RAF support. In the wake of the air assault, strong forces of German infantry attacked the villages held by the British troops, and before dark it became clear that these could no longer be held. Franklyn therefore decided that he had no option but to tell Martel to pull his troops back behind the 17th Infantry Brigade, which by this time had taken up a position roughly along the line of the River Scarpe west of Arras.

At the end of the day [Franklyn recorded], my uppermost feeling was one of bitter disappointment. I had been so hopeful earlier and now so little seemed to have been achieved. The capture of four hundred prisoners appeared a small reward for so much effort. I had, at the time, no conception of the extent to which the counter-attack around Arras had put the cat among the German pigeons. Yet I think that I should have appreciated the considerable moral effect that the Germans are subject to if their carefully laid plans are disrupted.

Throughout 22 May there was a lull in the fighting, providing a much needed respite that enabled the 13th and 17th Brigades to consolidate the defensive positions and the British artillery to make preparations to counter a renewed German offensive. Franklyn, concerned that the right flank of the 17th Infantry Brigade along the Scarpe to the west of Arras was insecure, arranged with General Prioux to station one of his armoured units there while Brigadier Churchill's 151st Infantry Brigade, which had borne the brunt of the fighting on the previous day and had suffered substantial casualties, was moved

to Vimy Ridge where the Canadians had fought so valiantly in
1917 and which dominated the whole area. Franklyn himself
had fought in the Arras area in 1916, and his knowledge of
the terrain proved invaluable in positioning his defensive
forces.

At dawn on 23 May, the British troops at Arras waited ner-
vously for the impending German attack. The main weight of
the assault was bound to fall on the 13th Infantry Brigade
which held a front some five thousand yards long, with the
Royal Inniskillings on the left from Plouvain to St Vaast, the
2nd Wiltshire on their right as far as Roeux, and the 2nd
Cameronians in reserve near Fresnes. Supporting artillery consisted of the 9th, 91st and 97th Field Regiments. The 17th
Infantry Brigade were in position to the west of the Arras road
around Maroeuil with a few tanks of the 1st French Light
Mechanized Division further to the west on Mont St Eloi.

The first attack was launched shortly after sunrise when an
enemy Infantry Brigade forced a passage across the river between the 13th and 150th Infantry Brigades, involving the 2nd
Royal Inniskillings and 2nd Wiltshires in heavy fighting. The
situation was saved by the 2nd Cameronians, who moved up
rapidly from their reserve position, and with their help the
assault was beaten off. Later in the day, the Cameronians took
up new positions on Vimy Ridge under the command of the
50th Division, while some of the British troops were actually
fighting in the old First World War trenches which were pre-
served as part of the Canadian memorial. These proved to be
a real boon, as many of the entrenching tools belonging to the
13th and 17th Brigades had been left on the motor transport,
and the men had nothing but their bare hands with which to
dig foxholes.

The 13th Brigade had successfully withstood the first assault;
it was soon to be the turn of the 17th Brigade. At 09.00 on the
23rd, the Brigade Commander, Brigadier Stopford, was carrying out a reconnaissance when he saw a large force of German
armour and about two hundred infantry moving up towards
Mont St Eloi. Ahead of the tanks, the German artillery laid

down a heavy barrage on the British positions, and this was followed by an attack against the 2nd Northamptons on the extreme right of the line. The Brigade Anti-Tank Company succeeded in knocking out one German tank, but then the blow fell. The small force of French tanks which was supposed to be protecting the right flank of the 17th Brigade, together with a French 75-mm field gun regiment at Ecurie, suddenly decided that they were badly needed elsewhere. Franklyn immediately went to find the commander of the French armoured group to try to encourage him to fight. He found the man lying drunk behind a haystack. Although Prioux later offered to have his subordinate replaced, it was clear to Franklyn that the French were not going to be of much further assistance.

At 14.30, German infantry infiltrated Maroueil Wood and were ejected only after a bitter hand to hand fight with the 2nd Northamptons. The Germans launched a second attack soon after, this time with tanks crashing their way through the trees, and a Mk IV got close enough to hit Brigade HQ with some highly accurate shell-fire. The German attacks grew in confidence, and towards the end of the afternoon 'C' Company of the 2nd Northamptons was overwhelmed. At 18.00 hours, with their right flank completely exposed following the dis- appearance of the French, the battalion was ordered to with- draw to Neuville St Vaast, where they were subjected to a very heavy air attack. In less than two days of fighting, they had sustained 352 casualties, including their commanding officer and several other senior officers.

During the evening, the enemy once again launched a strong attack against the 13th Infantry Brigade, the weight of the assault falling on the left flank of the 2nd Wiltshires. This time there was no reserve battalion to redress the situation, and the Germans succeeded in breaking through. Brigadier Dempsey, the Brigade Commander, was forced to pivot back on his left. Meanwhile, the 2nd Royal Inniskillings were hastily divided into two groups and ordered to form a brigade reserve at Raches. The battalion's transport, under the command of Major Vining, withdrew soon after dark under continual fire

E

and harassment by enemy patrols. The journey, over fields of mown hay, was a perilous one. On one occasion, the vehicles were held up by a German machine-gun nest. An NCO, Lance-Corporal Quigg, wormed his way forward alone and disposed of the gunners one by one with superb marksmanship, for which he was awarded a well-deserved Military Medal.

By 22.00 it was apparent that the situation had deteriorated to such an extent that Frankforce was in danger of being cut off. On its right the 17th Infantry Brigade had been pushed back to a line between Berthonnal Farm and Sainte Catherine, while what was left of the French had fallen back to Souchez. The 1st Army Tank Brigade had pulled back even further, behind the canal line. The 150th Infantry Brigade was still hanging on, albeit in some confusion, between Souchez and Vimy, while to the east of Arras the 151st and 13th Infantry Brigades were finding it increasingly difficult to hold their ground. In Arras itself the remains of Petreforce were almost completely surrounded.

Shortly before midnight, Franklyn received orders from Lord Gort to try to extricate Frankforce. It was easier said than done. Franklyn was now faced with the problem of extricating the equivalent of three divisions through an ever narrowing bottleneck. To complicate matters still further, most of the British troops were still in contact with the enemy, and only three to four hours of darkness remained. To move across unknown country at night would be almost impossible, and there were only two roads available. Of these the enemy was known to have crossed the one leading to Douai following their drive through the 13th Brigade, and there was no intelligence as to whether the road to Lens was still clear or not. Nevertheless, conscious that there was no time to be lost, Franklyn ordered all wheeled transport to move via Lens and all troops on foot by the Douai road, risking the possibility of having to fight their way through the Germans.

The withdrawal of the 5th and 50th Divisions from the Arras salient began shortly before midnight, the exhausted troops moving up the Douai road like ghosts, not speaking, heads bent and hardly noticing the steady stream of refugees moving into the opposite direction. The withdrawal was not molested, the Germans also being probably too exhausted to follow up their advantage, and although German aircraft were heard overhead, no bombs fell on the narrow lifeline along which the British troops tramped. The last to get away were the 150th Brigade and the garrison at Arras, which did not start until after daybreak on the 24th. With daylight they were able to move across country where they presented a good target for German aircraft, and they had a harder time of it than their counterparts who had got away during the night. Nevertheless, they came through with surprisingly few casualties.

Shortly after his arrival at Douai, General Franklyn was informed that the 5th and 50th Divisions were to co-operate with the French v Corps under the command of General Altmayer in a final counter-attack to try to close the gap which the Germans were extending with every passing day, by breaking through the over-stretched Panzer divisions and linking up with General Frère's new Sixth Army on the Somme. Details of the plan were to be disclosed at a conference convened that same morning by General Blanchard, who had taken over command from the late General Billotte of the French and British Armies in northern France. The new attack was scheduled for 26 May, the earliest possible date when it could be mounted in view of the necessary organization that had to go into it.

The following day, the 5th and 50th Divisions were already on their way southwards when they received new orders. With plans for Operation Dynamo – the evacuation of the BEF from the Channel ports – already well advanced and the British divisions in the process of pulling back towards the coast, Lord Gort, realizing the futility of the French plan – which had first been proposed by General Georges on 18 May and bandied about from one commander to another since then – decided to use both the British divisions in countering the threatening German attack through Belgium, where the progressive collapse of the Belgian Army had left a ten-mile-wide gap undefended by Allied troops. If this gap could not be closed, it would mean that the Germans could reach the Channel coast and in particular the port of Dunkirk unmolested, destroying all hope of evacuating the BEF successfully.

After some delay, Franklyn received his new orders from Lord Gort; they were to hold the Ypres-Comines Canal with the 5th and 50th Divisions. The dangerous gap lay on the left of General Brooke's II Corps, where there was nothing in the path of the three German divisions advancing through Belgium except a single British Brigade, the 143rd, holding a front of ten thousand yards along the line of the canal. Because of the delay in Franklyn's receiving his orders, it was touch and go whether the 5th and 50th Divisions would arrive in the line before the German spearheads. As the two divisions trudged northwards again, Franklyn issued his orders. The 143rd Brigade was to close in to its right and reduce the front to be defended to five thousand yards. The 13th Brigade, when it arrived, would take the centre sector of three thousand yards and the 17th Brigade would hold two thousand yards on the extreme left.

Franklyn set up his HQ in Ploegsteert Château, and at first light on 26 May he set out to reconnoitre the ground and confer with the Commander of the 143rd Brigade, which had just completed its movement to the right. Some time later, the 13th and 17th Brigades began to arrive only minutes ahead of the advance units of the German Sixth Army, which opened fire on the British troops as they were moving into their positions. The three-thousand-yard front of the 5th Division extended from a bend in the canal north of Hollebeke to Zillebeke, a village three miles south-east of Ypres, and the nature of the terrain compelled the positions to be sited mostly on forward slopes in full view of the enemy and open to heavy and accurate mortar and shell fire. The canal itself was quite useless as an anti-tank obstacle, being completely dry. There was one bright spot in a generally unfavourable situation: General Brooke had succeeded in securing the whole of the heavy and medium artillery of 1 Corps, which was now placed under Franklyn's command together with two regiments of field artillery. The French 1st Light Armoured Division was also supposed to be supporting the British line, but when Brigadier Stopford went to find them at Zillebeke, their last reported position, he found only a few tanks, and these were in the process of pulling out on their way to Ypres.

The 17th Infantry Brigade, with the 2nd Royal Scots Fusiliers on its right and the 6th Seaforths on its left along the railway line and the 2nd Northamptons in reserve on the west bank of the canal in thickly-wooded country, would therefore have to hold Zillebeke alone until the arrival of the 50th Division. On the right of 17th Infantry Brigade, 13th Infantry Brigade extended to Houtham where the 2nd Cameronians joined the 7th Royal Warwicks of 143rd Infantry Brigade. On their left were the 2nd Royal Inniskillings and in reserve the 2nd Wiltshires, holding the high ground eight hundred yards to the east of the St Eloi-Warneton road.

The German plan of attack called for an assault by the 18th, 31st and 61st Divisions of von Reichenau's Sixth Army against the British line, with the object of taking Kemmel and Poperinghe. The first major attack developed against Comines on 143rd Brigade's front on the morning of 27 May, and although the assault was not as well prepared as it might have been, the Germans succeeded in penetrating between the widely dispersed defensive positions. Some of the latter were completely surrounded but their garrisons continued to fight on, and throughout the rest of the day there was a confused mixture of British and German troops along 143rd Brigade's front. In one sense this was to the British advantage, for although the German artillery could not open fire for fear of hitting its own troops, the British artillery was able to break up several attacks by shelling German infantry forming up beyond the canal.

Realizing that there would be a complete lack of British air observation, Franklyn had lost no time in setting up a network of excellent observation posts which were able to direct the

artillery with great accuracy. To some extent, targets had to
be selected by guesswork, but Franklyn had so much artillery
at his disposal that whole areas could be blanketed. Nevertheless, continual enemy attacks steadily forced back 143rd Infantry Brigade, and this, together with a strong assault against
Houtham, another between the 2nd Cameronians and the 2nd
Royal Inniskillings and a third on Hollebeke, put 13th Infantry
Brigade in a difficult position by the early afternoon. Accordingly, at 16.00 hours, the Brigade Commander, Brigadier
Dempsey (later General Sir Miles Dempsey) ordered his forward battalions to withdraw to the high ground along the St
Eloi-Warneton road where the 2nd Wiltshires were in position.
This withdrawal was carried out under constant shellfire and
harassment by enemy patrols. Further to the north, 17th
Brigade had also been under heavy attack since 10.00 hours;
in this sector, relentless enemy pressure threw back the 6th
Seaforth Highlanders from their positions along the railway
line and almost surrounded the 2nd Royal Scots Fusiliers. By
13.00 hours both battalions had pulled back to the south of
the 2nd Northampton reserve position, which soon also found
itself under attack.

In the evening, the 150th Brigade of the 50th Division came
into line at Zillebeke, the remainder of the Division following
during the night to take up positions in and around Ypres.
Meanwhile, General Brooke had been making determined
efforts to secure other units to bolster the British line. These
included the 13th/18th Hussars, the 10th and 11th Infantry
Brigades and the Royal Engineers from the 4th Infantry Division and the 3rd Grenadier Guards, 2nd North Staffords and
2nd Sherwood Foresters, all drawn from the 1st Infantry Division. Franklyn, his left flank in a very precarious condition,
at once determined to use these fresh units to carry out a series
of determined counter-attacks in an effort to improve the situation on all three Brigade fronts before darkness.

Shortly afterwards, it was reported to Franklyn that the
commander of one of the new battalions, the 6th Black Watch,
was thirsting to make a counter-attack near Comines. Franklyn

ordered the attack to go ahead, supported by the light tanks of the 13th/18th Hussars. It began at 19.00 hours, and after heaving fighting the British succeeded in driving the enemy back to the Kortekeer River line, inflicting substantial casualties on them. Following this limited success, Franklyn decided to launch a bigger counter-attack on the right later that evening. It was to be carried out by the 3rd Grenadier Guards and the 2nd North Staffords and would go against all the rules in the book by advancing in the half-light over ground that had not been reconnoitred. Franklyn, however, felt that the risk was justifiable.

At 21.00 the two battalions, commanded by Lieutenant Colonels Alan Adair and Butterworth, fixed bayonets and moved off into the dusk. For the Germans, the sight of these determined men advancing towards them with bayonets at the ready was a considerable shock, and the British were on them before they could organize themselves. In the course of the advance, the right hand Company of the Grenadiers and some of the Black Watch joined forces with some of the 13th/18th Hussars and Engineers, still holding out in Comines after their earlier counter-attack, and they all advanced together. After heavy hand to hand fighting with considerable casualties on both sides, the Grenadiers and North Staffords had succeeded in throwing back the enemy and were firmly established on the Ypres-Comines Canal. Soon afterwards, the 11th Brigade of the 4th Division arrived in the line, and Franklyn stationed them behind the centre of the front on Wytschaete Ridge, which had been the scene of severe fighting during the First World War. During the night, General Montgomery's 3rd Division also arrived in the battle area, passing behind the British front and moving into position on the left of the 50th Division.

Franklyn planned to make a counter-attack with the aid of the 4th Division's 10th Brigade on the morning of 28 May, but before this could be implemented, the 18th German Division launched a heavy assault on the sector of the line held by the Grenadiers and the North Staffords, and although both battalions held out, they suffered more casualties than they had sustained during the counter-attack of the previous evening. Brigadier Dempsey's 13th Brigade also came under heavy attack, but here the line held, and the Germans received such a beating that there was no doubt that the British had obtained the best of the encounter. A subsequent counter-attack by the 10th Brigade sealed off the gaps created by the infiltration of the German 18th Division, and by nightfall the British line was solid once more.

At about this time, all officers of Company Commander level learned of the immediate evacuation of the British Expeditionary Force from Dunkirk. Only then was it fully realized how much the safety of the whole Expeditionary Force had depended on the gallant two-day defence of the Ypres-Comines Canal. Now that the imminent surrender of what remained of the Belgian Army in the North was certain, it was realized that this line of defence would soon become untenable, and at 22.00 hours on the 28th, orders were given for the units in the line to begin a gradual withdrawal. Last to leave were the artillery, moving out of their positions at 03.00 and taking up new stations near Kemmel. Before they left, they launched a thunderous barrage at the Germans with the object of preventing the latter from probing ahead in force. Nevertheless, while the 3rd and 50th Divisions swung back northwards on the pivot of Nordschote to form an intermediate line from Nordschote to Poperinghe, the 5th Division had a difficult time disengaging and was being heavily shelled and machine-gunned. It was only with extreme difficulty that the Division, reduced to little more than two battalions in strength after two days of severe fighting, managed to set up a temporary defensive position alongside 42nd Infantry Division on the line of the River Yser.

Only four miles behind Franklyn's gallant rearguard, the remainder of the British Expeditionary Force was struggling back along the narrow roads towards the perimeter of the allied bridgehead around Dunkirk, which ran from Gravelines through Bergues, Furnes and Nieuport. By nightfall on the 28th, the day on which Lord Gort had ordered the general withdrawal to the bridgehead, the British Divisions ran from right to left in this order: 46th, 42nd, 1st, 50th, 3rd and 4th. On the night of the 29th, most of the BEF's surviving vehicles and equipment were destroyed and the troops marched into the final perimeter in the sandhills around Moeres and Adin-kirk to join the long silent queues of men – exhausted, battle-shocked and famished – who shuffled their way along the beaches to embark in the armada of small craft that had come to their rescue.

The drama of that withdrawal and the agony of waiting that followed it was summed up tersely by an officer of the 4th Battalion the Green Howards, which had formed part of the 150th Brigade in the defence of the Ypres-Comines Line. It is a story that could have been told by any member of any of the units that took part in that epic last-ditch stand.

28 May
It rained hard in the early morning – the first rain since the German attack started. All was quiet both when I walked round the front during the night and before stand-to, but about 10.00 hours, when I was at Brigade, a message arrived that the enemy appeared to be attacking B of our other battalion from a southerly direction, and I was ordered to take charge of that flank while my B – still on the ramparts – would be under command of Lieutenant-Colonel Bush. I was told that the situation further to the right was very obscure, but the Northumberland Fusiliers were operating in that area, and I was to get into touch with them.

Without a map, it is not possible to describe correctly the moves and counter-moves of this day. The Germans attacked strongly along the length of the old canal but after an advance of perhaps two hundred yards, were held by our sister battalion, while A Com-pany succeeded in closing the gap between them and the Fusiliers. The carriers (now only five under Sergeant Cauchie) operated on the road on the right flank of A while the Fusiliers were being located. By 16.00, I was able to report to Brigade that the right flank was secure, but meanwhile the Germans began to advance against Trois Bois. Here they were held, though during the night they infiltrated to a small extent. At 18.00 hours, orders were received from Brigade to prepare to withdraw in our own MT to an

E*

area just north of Poperinghe after destroying all surplus kit and
stores. These orders were a complete surprise to us. No one had
heard of the rumours of the impending evacuation of the BEF or
that King Leopold had surrendered. But when the Quartermaster
came up to Ypres at midnight, with an empty B Echelon, rumours
became facts, and he told us of the destruction of stores and equipment at Dickebusch: of other units falling back on Dunkirk.

29 May
The timings for the withdrawal were not received until the very
early hours, and although I had company representatives standing
by, I felt that it was bound to be a daylight withdrawal. At 03.30
hours, the first parties reported to me on their way to the Transport, lying up just west of Ypres. By 05.00 hours, all had reported
except Second Lieutenant Booth and a small detachment of c
Company whom PSM Fenwick was unable to find. Thinking that
either they had been killed, captured or had withdrawn through
Ypres, I drove off in my carrier along the Ypres-Poperinghe road
(Second Lieutenant Booth actually did not withdraw until 09.00
hours, when he rejoined us at Poperinghe). And so we became part
of the rearguard of the BEF.

I took up the defensive position north of Poperinghe with A
Company on the right, c remnant in the centre, D on the left with
B in reserve, behind Battalion HQ, in a farm surrounded by hop-
poles. The 151st Brigade were on our left, and I was told that the
1st Corps were on our right. It was not until the afternoon that
two German armoured cars bumped our forward posts and captured a platoon of A Company. At 18.00 hours, I was summoned
to Brigade to receive orders for a further withdrawal to Moeres,
and was told that the 1st Corps on our right had already withdrawn: I was to send my carriers out on the right to get in touch
with the Fusiliers: during the withdrawal they and 14/18 DGs
were to cover us.

Withdrawals were becoming rather a drill now, and I told my
companies to report to me by a shrine some three hundred yards
behind Battalion HQ: they would then embus in what was left of
our MT about a mile further back. While preparations for the withdrawal were in progress, the Germans established a post on the
right of A Company and subjected Battalion HQ to rifle fire and
shelling from a close support gun.

Towards dusk, the companies withdrew as arranged, again without casualty and without pursuit. The withdrawal was covered first of all by the Fusiliers and subsequently by my three remaining carriers.

30 May

The journey to Moeres was very slow: the roads were congested with MT and blocked in places with abandoned transport: there were few maps and these only 1/250,000: the route had not been reconnoitred: the MT drivers were tired out. So it was not surprising that part of the convoy led by the Padre, MO Second Lieutenant Goellnicht and the RSM went astray. Captain Mansell and I and the three carriers got lost too. At last, seeing a dim light in a village, I sent Mansell to find out our whereabouts, and discovered that the village was Isenberghe, and the Colonel of the Regiment, General Franklyn, was within. He gave us much-needed refreshment. And so by way of Houthem to Moeres, where I found Major Cooke-Collis awaiting our arrival by a cross roads which were soon to become very unhealthy. My first orders were to lie up in a farm at Moeres where I was to be in brigade reserve, but at 09.15 hours, I was ordered to move the Battalion forward to fill a gap between the Duke of Wellingtons on the right and East Yorkshires on the left along the line of the Bergues-Furnes canal. My right was exactly on the Belgian frontier and my left by the Houthem canal bridge exclusive. I put B Company on the right with D on the left: the remainder of A in support and C combined with HQ in reserve by Battalion HQ at Westmoerhoek. Each company had a canal or ditch in front of them, and the rich arable fields all around were very rapidly becoming flooded. Again I had a tremendous front of about 1¾ miles. The Battalion worked hard digging slit trenches all day, and when it was dark, working parties from the South Staffordshire Regiment came up to help.

31 May

Today the Germans attacked on our right and left: they secured a foot-hold over the bridge on our right after a fierce mortar bombardment of the 'Dukes'. B Company came in for some of the 'overs'. D also experienced some sniping but our reply both with rifle and artillery fire was effective; the men were well dug in and the casualties were very few. It was B Echelon who got the worst

of it, as they were constantly shelled and bombed out of every
place in which they chose to lie up. They lost several men but no
trucks, and when orders were received to withdraw and go into a
bivouac area astride the road Adinkerne-Dunkirk and road running south from Bray Dunes, the MTO produced the necessary
transport. This brigade order, oo No. 6, dated 31 May 1940, is the
sole survivor. In the method paragraph, the timings were:

(a) Thinning out of Rifle Battalions will commence
   at 01.30 hours
(b) Line of FDLs will be evacuated at 02.30 hours

and in paragraph 9, the forward battalions were ordered to establish a covering line with their carrier platoons just north of the
road from 378818 to 407824 behind their battalion areas. Carriers
were to be in position by 01.00 hours.

1 June

And so once more we withdrew. Moeres we had to avoid, and the
route for part of the way was across fields and cart tracks, and even
these had been shelled and bombed. Just before turning right over
the canal to Dunkirk, the police directed all transport into a field
on the left of the road. Here it was parked neatly – and burned or
rendered useless.

South of Bray Dunes over the canal in a field on the left of the
road, we dispersed and dug in. The QM produced meals somehow
(we had now been on half rations for some days), and we were
bombed but had only one casualty: we watched air battles and
saw several Nazi planes shot down.

At 15.00 hours, when I was thinking that the next move would
be to the UK, the Brigadier sent for me to his HQ in Bray Dunes to
give me orders to stabilize the line around Ghyvelde and to the
left: to link up with the KSLI and possibly the French. So southwards we marched again over roads that were rapidly becoming
awash with flooding.

After a quick reconnaissance with Major Pegler (RE), who was
to help in the preparation of defences, I sent A Company forward
on the right to St François cross roads, and c on the left to an un-
named road junction. B in support on the right in Ghyvelde and D
in support on the left with orders to get in touch with the French,
which Second Lieutenant Nuttall and Maalaud (our Liaison agent)
succeeded in doing.

Positions had barely been taken up when we received orders at 20.30 hours to withdraw to Dunkirk and embark for the UK. Meanwhile the MTO and Second Lieutenant Booth (C Company) had not been idle. Second Lieutenant Pendred had salvaged enough transport to embus the Battalion, while C had collected their own MT to bring them to Ghyvelde. Unfortunately C had to debus earlier than expected as the bridge over the canal at Ghyvelde was blown under C's noses when they were the wrong side of it. Quickly the French manned the right side, and I had the greatest difficulty in making them cease fire in order to enable C to wade across.

And so by MT to Dunkirk with the skies lit up by burning dumps, the road lined with deserted transport, the odd shell screaming overhead. Travelling along in the rear of the Battalion, some telephone wires in Dunkirk became wound round the wheels of my 8 cwt truck, and I saw the convoy ahead of me vanish into the darkness. After driving around Dunkirk docks, it was nearly dawn before I at last connected with the Mole to find troops moving back from the Mole on to the beach – and here again I found the Battalion.

Meanwhile Major Cooke-Collis, guided by an RASC officer, had led the Battalion through Dunkirk, debussed and joined the masses of troops who were moving slowly on to the Mole.

2 June

The Head of the Battalion had almost reached the boats when the order was given to about turn as no more boats would leave that morning. So the Battalion made their way back to the beach and dug in. Four unlucky shells at the base of the Mole killed Second Lieutenant Wilby and several ORs and wounded many more.

And so, from 03.00 hours to 21.00 hours, we sat in holes or cellars and slept and ate and waited. During this period, Dunkirk was frequently bombed, and parts of it became a roaring furnace. Luckily but few bombs fell on the beach and we suffered no casualties. At 21.00 hours, we formed up in fours by the water's edge and moved slowly on to the Mole through the regulating compound arranged by Brigadier Haydon.

Operation Dynamo, the evacuation of the British Expeditionary Force from Dunkirk, began in earnest on 26 May and ended at 14.23 hours on 4 June, according to the official Admiralty

timing. During that nine-day period the incredible total of
337,000 men were brought out, 140,000 of them French troops.

Much has been written on the 'deliverance of Dunkirk', and
a deep appraisal of it is not within the scope of this work.
There are, however, several factors which need to be considered in the context of the campaign as a whole. First of all,
on 24 May – a day on which enemy attacks were pressed home
with great severity all along the shrinking Allied perimeter,
the British pulled back from Arras, and the armour of Reinhardt
and Guderian seemed all set for a final drive on Dunkirk after
capturing several bridgeheads on the Aa Canal – the Panzers
suddenly halted on Hitler's orders. To the Panzer leaders, this
move came as a profound shock. Guderian wrote: 'Hitler
ordered the left wing to stop on the Aa. It was forbidden to
cross that stream. We were not informed of the reason for
this. The order contained the words: "Dunkirk is to be left to
the Luftwaffe." We were utterly speechless.'

A lot of explanations were subsequently given for this
famous 'Halt Befehl', ranging from the possibility that Hitler
wanted to provide the British with a face-saving outlet to encourage them to enter peace negotiations (a highly improbable
notion, yet one which historians have persistently clung to,
despite the fact that there is no evidence to support it) to the
theory that the terrain in front of Dunkirk was unsuitable for
armoured operations. What is factual is that, on 23 May,
Hermann Göring rang up Hitler with the boast that the Luftwaffe could finish the job in the Dunkirk pocket single-handed,
and this was undoubtedly fresh in Hitler's mind when, the
following morning, he met Rundstedt at the latter's HQ in
Charleville to discuss the problems that the offensive had so
far encountered.

Rundstedt told the Führer that he was still worried about
the security of the advance's southern flank, particularly as
there was still the chance of a French counter-offensive developing from the south of the Somme. The British attack at
Arras had also come as a severe shock, and in its wake von
Kleist had reported that fifty per cent of his armour was un-

serviceable, although much of it only temporarily. It would therefore be too much of a risk to subject what remained of the armour to the possibility of a further mauling by the British Tank Brigade in the marshy terrain before Dunkirk, for the timetable for the offensive called for a maximum concentration of the Panzer divisions in just over a week's time to launch the second phase of the offensive, against the French armies south of the Somme. This had to be given overall priority – and besides, it was only a question of time before the encircled Allied forces in the north were compelled to surrender.

Hitler agreed with these observations; above all, the armour had to be rested and brought up to strength again in readiness for the new drive to the south. So the order went out for the tanks to halt, and it was two days before it was rescinded – two days of respite that enabled the British to gear up the evacuation and so avert what would have amounted to the virtual death of their army.

Even when the order for the tanks to move again was finally given at 12.00 hours on 26 May, it took sixteen hours to put it into full effect. In the meantime, four British divisions and a substantial number of French troops had succeeded in escaping from a potential trap at Lille, where they would undoubtedly have been cut off by the advance of 7th Panzer if the armour had not been halted, and these eventually contributed towards the establishment of a strong defensive perimeter around Dunkirk. They were lucky; when the armour got on the move again, the trap closed and the Panzers sealed off thirty-five thousand French troops of the First Army in Lille. Under the command of General Molinié, they fought on for four days, but under the combined onslaught of the 4th, 5th and 7th Panzers, they were eventually forced to surrender.

Meanwhile, even before the Halt Order came into effect, Guderian's armoured and motorized columns had been subjected to considerable delays when, in their drive northwards to Dunkirk along the coast, they encountered spirited resistance at Boulogne and Calais. Boulogne, which was cut off on 22 May, was heroically defended for thirty-six hours by two

British Guards battalions, a handful of French territorial troops and five naval gun batteries before the garrison was evacuated by sea in the early hours of the 24th, having lost two hundred men. At Calais, Churchill ordered the garrison – consisting of a battalion of the Rifle Brigade, one of the 60th Rifles, the Queen Victoria Rifles and a battalion of the Royal Tank Regiment with twenty-one light and twenty-seven cruiser tanks, together with an equal number of French troops – to fight to the death. Under the command of Brigadier Nicholson, the garrison fought one of the bravest last-ditch actions in the annals of the British Army before it was finally overwhelmed on the 26th.

The gallant resistance of Boulogne and Calais – just as much as Hitler's *Halt Befehl* – was a major contributory factor to the success of Operation Dynamo. When the Germans finally launched their attack by land on the Dunkirk perimeter on 1 June, they encountered well-prepared defences which proved almost impossible to break, and what small gains were made were lost again when the Allies counter-attacked later in the day. The attacks intensified on the 2nd, but once again the Germans made little or no progress. At the eastern end of the perimeter, one attack was completely shattered by the 8th Zouaves and the 150th Infantry Regiment, while at the other end of the line, an assault by Hubicki's 9th Panzer was shrivelled up by French 75s, firing over open sights. The French perimeter forces fought on until the night of the 3rd, when they began to fall back progressively towards the beaches for evacuation. Fifty-three thousand men were taken off by the British evacuation fleet that night, and the following morning the first Panzers rolled into the town. The defence of Dunkirk was over.

Meanwhile, the French counter-attack from the south – which both Hitler and Rundstedt had feared – had ended in failure and fiasco. While the French Tenth Army concentrated opposite the bridgeheads that had been established by the Germans on the Somme, the 2nd and 5th Cavalry Divisions, together with two brigades of the 1st British Armoured Division, which had recently arrived in France, were ordered to attack the enemy bridgeheads at Abbeville and St Valéry. The counter-attack was launched on 26 May and was over almost before it had started. The British 2nd Brigade, with its light five-ton tanks, encountered heavy and accurate anti-tank fire, and the 10th Hussars and Queen's Bays lost sixty-five AFVs in an hour, together with a further fifty-five which broke down. The French 5th Cavalry, with the 2nd and 5th Royal Tank Regiments, managed to take Saigneville between Abbeville and St Valéry, but there they were halted by minefields and heavy gunfire.

The newly-promoted General de Gaulle's 4th Armoured Division, which arrived in the area from the Aisne on the 28th, had more success. With 140 tanks supported by three artillery groups, thirty-seven anti-tank guns, two battalions of dismounted dragoons, the 4th Chasseurs, an armoured car squadron of the 10th Cuirassiers and the 22nd Colonial Infantry Regiment, de Gaulle attacked northwards on the 29th, crossing the Rouen road and making some small gains at the cost of heavy casualties. A second attack was launched on the 30th, but it was stopped dead by withering fire from German 88-mms. By the morning of the 31st, the 2nd, 5th and 4th Divisions had only forty serviceable tanks between them, and the battered 4th armoured was withdrawn to rest and refit. It was destined to take no further major part in the battle. A few days later, de Gaulle himself was appointed Under-Secretary of State at the War Office, leaving the front for Paris – and his destiny.

CHAPTER 6   **The Last Offensive**

As the battered remnants of the BEF sailed from Dunkirk, the Wehrmacht divisions that had speared across the drab plains of Belgium and Flanders now wheeled southwards to form an unbroken line that stretched for two hundred miles along the northern banks of the Somme, the Ailette and the Aisne. Across the river line, the 140 divisions of Army Groups A and B – the Panzers now rested and refreshed after their six-day respite following Hitler's *Halt Befehl* at Dunkirk – faced, from west to east, the Tenth, Seventh, Sixth, Second and Third French Armies, forming the Weygand Line extending from the sea to Verdun. They comprised a total of forty-nine divisions.

Both sides had lost heavily in the three weeks' battle in the north. German figures of killed, wounded and missing stood at over sixty-one thousand officers and men, while French losses amounted to 370,000 men – including the vast number of prisoners – of the First, Seventh and Ninth Armies. In material terms, too, France's material losses had been crippling. They amounted to a quarter of her field artillery, a third of her armour and most of her transport.

For the last phase of the Battle of France – codenamed '*Fall Rot*' ('Plan Red') – the Germans had assembled the full weight of their armour; ten Panzer divisions, formed into five corps each with two divisions. The brunt of the offensive was to be borne by Hoth's XV Corps, which was to drive forward on the western flank between Amiens and the sea; von Kleist's Armoured Group comprising XXXIX and XLI Panzer Corps, with the task of pushing across the Somme towards Amiens and Péronne in the central sector; and, further east, Guderian's two Panzer Corps, which were to spear southwards from the Aisne.

While the German divisions gathered their strength for the coming assault, it was the Luftwaffe's turn to strike. On 1 and 2 June, fog and drizzle covering the whole of France brought a temporary halt to air operations on both sides, but on the morning of the 3rd the weather cleared and a massive armada of five hundred bombers and fighters drawn from Luftflotten 2 and 5 took off from their German bases and converged on a single objective – Paris. The attack, code-named 'Operation Paula', was to have the twofold objective of dealing a crippling blow at French morale and destroying as many as possible of the Armée de l'Air's combat aircraft and airfields as a preliminary to the coming German land offensive.

The French fighter squadrons, which had been hurriedly redeployed in the Paris area during the two-day respite, threw their dwindling resources against the overwhelming enemy formations, their pilots showing great heroism as they pressed home their attacks through the umbrella of Messerschmitts – some 250 aircraft drawn from five fighter Geschwader. In the course of the day's air battles, the French pilots destroyed twenty-six enemy aircraft, flying 243 sorties. Seventeen French fighters were shot down in combat and twelve pilots killed.

For the Luftwaffe, the results of Operation Paula were disappointing. The concentrated attacks on thirteen airfields in the Paris area had resulted in the destruction of only sixteen French aircraft on the ground, with a further seven damaged. Six runways had been temporarily put out of action, twenty-one vehicles destroyed and thirty-two personnel killed. All the bases attacked were serviceable again within forty-eight hours. The bombers had also attacked twenty-two railway stations and junctions; here, too, repairs had been effected by dawn on 4 June. Fifteen factories were hit, but only three suffered more than minor damage. The civilian death toll stood at 254, with 652 injured.

The German plan to isolate the city – which they intended

to bypass on both sides – by air attack was consequently a failure, and served in no way to lighten the task of the German ground forces. The latter went into action at dawn on 5 June, preceded by a massive artillery barrage along a 120-mile stretch of front from Laon to the Channel coast. As the shellfire lifted, von Bock's infantry and armour struck hard at the formations of General Besson's Third Army Group, which included the British 51st Highland Division under General Fortune and the 1st Armoured Division, the latter equipped mainly with lightly-armoured cruiser tanks and at only about one-third strength following the disastrous actions at the end of May. Reinforcements were on their way in the shape of the 52nd Lowland Division, which was beginning to arrive in Normandy, and the 1st Canadian Division, which was still in the British Isles. It was now apparent that they would be too late.

On the left of the Allied line, the 51st Division's 154th Brigade found itself under heavy attack from the direction of St Valéry, where the Germans had established a bridgehead on the Somme, and was gradually forced to withdraw from the defensive positions that had been hurriedly set up among the villages and woods between the river and the sea. On the right, the 153rd Brigade and the French 31st Alpine Division were also thrown back, withdrawing to the line of the River Bresle between Eu and Blangy. Further right still, the Germans struck hard out of the Abbeville bridgehead against the Dismounted Dragoons of the 2nd Cavalry Division, pushing them back towards Hallencourt where the 5th Cavalry was in position.

Although compelled to withdraw gradually, the French fought hard, contesting every yard of ground, and inflicted substantial casualties on the enemy. Between Condé and Hangest, the Germans found two railway bridges intact across the Somme, and on the night of 4/5 June, these were captured by units of Hoth's xv Panzer Corps. The German infantry pushed straight on to attack and overwhelm two Senegalese regiments of the 5th Colonial Division, creating a dangerous gap through which the Panzers drove towards Le Quesnoy. Pausing only to shoot up a few isolated pockets of resistance,

Rommel's 7th Panzer thundered on through Le Quesnoy into the Laudon Valley, where they were engaged by a group of 75-mm guns of the 72nd Artillery Regiment. Several German tanks were knocked out, but the remainder encircled the artillery group and progressively destroyed it. By nightfall on the 5th, Rommel had advanced so far that they had crossed the Luftwaffe's bomb line, and there was a danger that they would be attacked in error by their own dive-bombers at first light. He accordingly halted them and consolidated, waiting for the rest of the offensive to catch up.

By his daring thrust across country, Rommel had succeeded in making nonsense of the whole defensive policy of the Weygand Line. This relied not on a continuous front but on a network of 'hedgehogs' dotted over the countryside – each hedgehog being a fortified natural obstacle such as a village, wood or farmhouse, with the defending troops well dug in and supported by heavy machine-guns, mortars and 75-mms, the latter with the task of engaging the enemy armour over open sights. Wherever possible, each hedgehog was situated in a position that enabled it to provide covering fire for its neighbours, and each was provided with sufficient stores and ammunition to carry on fighting for a time even after it had been surrounded.

Although the Weygand Line had been designed to give some semblance of a defence in depth, it was by no means proof against a strong armoured thrust of the type in which Rommel specialized. It might have been a different story if the line had been backed up by strong forces of French armour and heavy air support, but it had neither. Nevertheless, by the end of the first day's fighting, Weygand's system appeared to be working; Weygand had ordered his forces to stand and fight to the death, and in many instances the French troops did precisely that. This time there was no disorganized rabble, streaming away from the front; this time the French were fighting with a valour born of desperation, conscious that they were the last shield between the armoured lance and their country's heart. Time and again, the French gunners refused to abandon their positions, hurling shell after shell at the Panzers until the steel tracks ground over them or the Stukas' bombs pounded them into the dust. At Amiens and Péronne, they halted the advance of von Kleist's Panzers after only a few miles; only in Rommel's sector had any significant progress been made.

The German bridgeheads were also attacked repeatedly by the French Air Force and the AASF, the latter now operating from bases in the Le Mans area with seventy Fairey Battles, and by about 250 aircraft of RAF Bomber Command, flying from Britain. On 5 June, the French day bombers and ground attack aircraft flew 126 sorties and dropped sixty tons of bombs; by this time the LeO 451s and Breguet 693s had been joined by American-built Martin 167s and Douglas DB-7s, although these were available only in small numbers. Ten bombers were lost during the day, but their fighter escorts destroyed seven Messerschmitts.

The following day von Kleist renewed his advance, but once again the French stopped him. One of his corps, XXXIX, had over half its force of armour disabled after two days of fighting. Once again, it was Rommel who kept the offensive going. Exploiting the gap he had created, he raced on to cover another thirty miles on the 6th, advancing as far as Forges-les-Eaux on the Beauvais-Dieppe road and slicing Altmayer's Tenth Army in two as he did so. On the 7th his meteoric progress continued as he drove the centre of the Tenth Army before him in what was fast becoming a rout, and at 02.00 on the 8th, after a brief halt, his tanks reached Elbeuf on the River Seine. In the picturesque villages, many inhabitants gazed in bewilderment as the Panzers rolled through, unable to comprehend the speed with which disaster was overtaking them. Only a few hours before, they had cheered and thrown bouquets of flowers at the men of their own 3rd Armoured Division, now pulling back over the Seine. Such was the confusion that in Elbeuf a woman came up to Rommel's command vehicle and asked the General if he was English.

Rommel's dash did not succeed in securing the Seine bridges, which were blown one after the other. The town of Rouen, however, fell that same morning to von Hartlieb's 5th Panzer, the tanks and personnel carriers rumbling in a long column up Autoroute 28 and entering the town unmolested. On Rommel's other flank, the xxxviii Infantry Corps under General Erich von Manstein had succeeded in forcing a passage through to the Lower Seine.

The Panzers' thrust to the Seine, and the splitting of the French Tenth Army, had effectively sealed off the French ix Corps – which included the 51st Highland Division – in the Rouen-Dieppe pocket, with their backs to the sea, and their encirclement was completed on the 9th when the 5th and 7th Panzer swung north-westwards from the Seine. Major-General Fortune, on learning that Rouen had fallen, at once pulled back the 51st Division and the 31st Alpine Division towards Le Havre, leaving a small force to cover the withdrawal. The following morning, Rommel, von Hartlieb and the 2nd Motorized Division made a concerted attack on ix Corps, which had set up a hasty line of defence around the perimeter of St Valéry-en-Caux, where the 51st Division and the remnants of the French forces expected to be evacuated by sea. This, however, was prevented by fog and by the Germans themselves, who by noon on the 11th were in a position to shell both the allied ships and the St Valéry beaches. The Highlanders and most of the French now had less than half a day's rations left. On the morning of the 12th, General Ihler, the ix Corps commander, ordered the French forces at St Valéry to surrender, and although this raised bitter protests from the Highlanders, who were prepared to fight on, they were compelled to do likewise soon afterwards. Over eight thousand British troops fell into the German net; the total bag of Allied troops that day was forty thousand, including no fewer than twelve generals.

Rommel's tanks clattered into Le Havre on the morning of the 14th. There they rested for forty-eight hours before pushing on towards Cherbourg, covering as much as 150 miles in a single day. There was no longer any opposition, and on 19 June, Rommel accepted Cherbourg's surrender. For the incredible 7th Panzer Division, which alone had taken close on a hundred thousand prisoners in its headlong dash from the Meuse to the sea, the Battle of France was over.

Meanwhile, on 9 June, Rundstedt's Army Group A had launched its attack on schedule on the Aisne, the weight of its offensive falling on the newly-formed Army Group Four, which comprised the Second, Fourth and Sixth Armies and was commanded by General Huntziger. Ever since the German breakthrough on the Meuse, the French Second Army had been under relentless pressure, striving – together with the left flank of the Third Army – to hold some sort of line between the Bar and Meuse and prevent the outflanking of the Maginot Line. Losses were heavy, particularly in General Flavigny's XXI Corps, and reserves were continually being drained to make good the attrition. Despite this, the Second Army had been compelled to withdraw during the last week in May, and as a consequence part of the Maginot defences – in the Montmédy sector – had to be abandoned.

Now, effective from 6 June, Huntziger's new Army Group Four – into the building of which the last reserves had been poured – was given the task of holding the Aisne from Montmédy to Attichy. Three days later, they received the full weight of the German attack, which was carried out by the Armoured Groups of Guderian and von Kleist, the latter having been switched eastwards after the French held it south of Amiens and Péronne.

This time, the infantry were to go in first and secure bridge-heads across the Aisne before the armour was committed. The first assault fell between Neufchâtel and Attigny, where the line was held by General de Lattre de Tassigny's 14th Division and Klopfenstein's 2nd Division. The French resisted furiously, and by the end of the day the Germans had succeeded in establishing only one small bridgehead near Château-Porcien. The Germans made determined attacks on de Lattre's 14th Division through the murk – partly mist, partly the effects of smoke shells – that lay like a veil across the Aisne Valley, but the French broke them all and took eight hundred prisoners into the bargain.

French losses, however, had been severe, and it was plain that Army Group Four would not be able to stem the German breakthrough for much longer. That night, Guderian pushed armour over into the solitary bridgehead, and the next morning elements of the 1st Panzer Division probed out through the French advance positions supported by heavy air strikes. Village after village went up in flames, and although the tanks made slow progress, the defenders were compelled to withdraw gradually. Then, in the early afternoon, the Panzers encountered units of the French 3rd Armoured Division, comprising ten B tanks and two battalions of Hotchkiss, the 42nd and 45th. German reconnaissance aircraft had warned of the approach of the French armour, and when the tanks reached Juneville, the German anti-tank gunners were ready for them. Six Hotchkiss were knocked out in as many minutes, and although the Bs made some progress, the French counter-attack – which lacked both artillery and air support – quickly petered out, though not before it had inflicted some casualties on Guderian's forces.

The situation continued to deteriorate, and in the early hours of 11 June, the French Second and Fourth Armies began to disengage, moving back through the forest of Belval towards the River Marne. The manœuvre was carried out only with extreme difficulty, for by this time both the XXXIX and XLI Panzer Corps had crossed the Aisne and were pushing southwards at speed, trapping some French units and destroying them. It was now clear that French resistance on the Aisne was practically at an end; by nightfall on the 11th, the German armour had reached Reims and a few hours later, Guderian's tanks took Chalons-sur-Marne, establishing a bridgehead on the river.

With Rouen captured in the west and the Marne crossed in the east, Paris was now threatened from west and north, with the leading German forces only fifty miles from the capital. Immediately north of Paris, bitter fighting raged in the forest of Compiègne, where the 11th 'Iron' Division sacrificed itself to buy time while the Seventh Army fell back to the Oise. In

Paris itself, the thunder of distant gunfire could be clearly heard, and the roads leading south were crowded with the inevitable tide of refugees – among it the French Government, which was departing for a safer location at Tours. On the 11th, aware that there was no hope of saving the capital, Weygand declared Paris an open city.

Meanwhile, the French fought to hold their last line of defence on the lower Seine. Weygand had committed all his available reserves to the battle, including two fresh divisions from North Africa. At the same time, the first contingent of a new British Expeditionary Force – the 52nd Lowland Division and part of the 1st Canadian – was landed at Cherbourg, commanded by General Brooke, formerly of 11 Corps. The 157th Brigade of the Lowland Division was immediately sent up to bolster the French line at Evreux, but when Brooke arrived at the French GHQ on the 12th – with no clear idea of the true situation – he was horrified to find that the French position was quite untenable. He at once contacted the War Office and gave his views, and on the 13th – after Churchill had intervened – he was ordered to prepare the withdrawal and evacuation of all British forces from France.

By nightfall on the 13th, the French forces in the west – the Seventh and Tenth Armies and the Armée de Paris, the latter formed originally to defend the capital to the last – were all in retreat towards the Loire. That same evening, units of Küchler's Eighteenth Army came within sight of the Eiffel Tower.

At 03.40 the next morning, a lone German motor-cyclist roared across the deserted Place Voltaire in the 11th Arrondissement, circled and went back the way he had come. As the hours went by, detachments of German troops, mostly from the 87th Infantry Division, began to appear all over the capital. Loudspeaker cars toured the streets, warning what was left of the population to stay indoors and await further instructions. Nevertheless, as the morning wore on, a few inhabitants began to trickle on to the streets, braving the thin drizzle to watch the seemingly endless column of German troops, armour and transport that rumbled southwards across Paris.

At 09.30, the German flag broke over the Arc de Triomphe. Fifteen minutes later, the hard-bitten, veteran troops of General von Koch-Erpach's 8th Infantry Division – part of Kluge's Fourth Army – marched down the Champs Elysées in a triumphal victory parade. As the field-grey columns passed the Tomb of the Unknown Warrior, with its Eternal Flame, they saluted. It was as much a gesture of total, overwhelming victory as one of homage.

At six-thirty that evening, the German soldiers clustered round the Arc de Triomphe like peacetime tourists were astonished to see two elderly Frenchmen marching towards them in full dress uniform, complete with swords. They were Edmond Ferrand and Charles Gaudin, both veterans of the First World War and both holding the honoured position of Guardians of the Flame. Instinctively, the Germans snapped to attention as the two men solemnly extinguished the Flame that had burned without interruption for almost twenty years. Then Ferrand and Gaudin marched away, the tears glistening on their cheeks in the evening sunlight.

The play was almost done now. In the east, the day after Paris fell, the fortress of Verdun – that symbol of French resistance, where the flower of the French army had bled in 1916 – was captured after less than a day's fighting. Elsewhere, the Germans were pushing forward relentlessly along the picturesque roads of France; Rommel raced down the road from Le Havre to Cherbourg, Guderian's armour took St Dizier, and on the 15th the 1st Panzer reached Gray-sur-Saône in the foothills of the Jura. On the upper Seine, von Kleist's tanks rolled into Dijon, completing the isolation of the Maginot Line and the four hundred thousand men manning its defences. The latter held their positions until the bitter end – until, in fact, they were told to lay down their arms by senior French officers acting on behalf of the Germans.

As the rout continued, the French Government – now at Bordeaux – found itself with a dilemma : whether to carry on the struggle from North Africa or to negotiate with the Germans for a cessation of hostilities. Since most of the surviving French air squadrons were already evacuating across the Mediterranean, the majority of the French ministers were in favour of a capitulation by the land forces – a proposal that Weygand hotly opposed. The British Government was also opposed to the idea of a French armistice unless orders were given immediately for the substantial French fleet in the Mediterranean to sail for British bases. The whole situation collapsed in total confusion. On the one hand there was the strong lobby of pro-armistice ministers, led by Marshal Pétain; on the other was Churchill's new proposal for a union between France and Britain, to carry on the fight to the bitter end. Finally, Reynaud resigned, and his place was taken by Pétain. In the evening of 16 June, the Spanish Ambassador was approached with a request that his government intervene on France's behalf and begin negotiations with the Germans for the end of hostilities and the drafting of peace terms.

At noon on 20 June, Pétain received instructions from the Germans by radio to send a French armistice delegation to Tours, where a temporary ceasefire had been arranged. On its arrival at Tours, the delegation, led by General Huntziger, was driven to Compiègne near Paris, there to be confronted by a triumphant Adolf Hitler and the famous *wagon-lit* in which, in November 1918, Marshal Foch and Weygand himself had received the representatives of a defeated Germany. There the terms of the armistice were thrashed out, and the document itself was signed at Réthondes on Saturday, 22 June. The ceasefire was to take effect at 00.35 hours on the 25th.

So it was over – almost. For France, the final stab in the back had come on 10 June, while her battered armies continued to fight on the Seine and the Aisne. On that day Mussolini's Italy, eager for its share of the spoils, declared war on the Allies. Thirty-two divisions were concentrated on France's Alpine Front and now they moved forward to the attack, confident of overwhelming the thinly-spaced French defences by sheer weight of numbers.

They were destined to receive a harsh rebuff. When, with

the French armies rapidly collapsing on 13 June, General Weygand had called for 'one last battle to save honour', the Alpine Front had been furthest from his mind. Yet it was here, amid the snow and the rarefied air of the mountains, that the battle was fought.

CHAPTER 7

Battle in the Alps

Between September 1939 and 10 June 1940, the day when Italy declared war on France, the combat effectives of the French Armée des Alpes were progressively whittled away to meet the demands of other sectors. By 10 June the original complement of 550,000 troops had been reduced to 175,000, of which 85,000 were first-line troops. Of this total, 4,500 were in position on the Swiss frontier; there remained, therefore, 80,500 men to confront the Italians, divided among two mountain divisions – the 64th and 65th – one standard infantry division, the 66th, and seven fortress demi-brigades entrusted with the defence of three fortified sectors: Savoie, Dauphiné and Alpes-Maritimes.

Opposing the French were three Italian armies divided into six Army Corps comprising thirty-four divisions, of which twenty-six were first-line and eight in reserve: a total of more than half a million men. The disparity was therefore serious, and both the Italian and German General Staffs believed that the French would be unable to hold out for very long in the face of a determined Italian general offensive in the Alps.

French and Italian patrols had made frequent contact with one another since the outbreak of war in September 1939. In the beginning such encounters had been characterized by strictly correct behaviour and even friendliness; in the spring of 1940, however, when Italian reconnaissance aircraft began to overfly the French positions and it became apparent that the Italians were building up their front-line forces, both sides shunned direct contact with one another. In May, just before the start of the German offensive, French patrols reported that a constant stream of tanks and ammunition convoys was reaching the Italian front-line positions, and on the 20th of that month, General Orly, commanding the Armée des Alpes, indicated that the Italians were capable of launching a general offensive at any time. Further intelligence that reached the French up to 9 June strengthened the belief that such an operation was imminent; at 18.00 hours the following day Mussolini declared war on France, with hostilities scheduled to begin at midnight.

With the exception of the heavily fortified positions – which were to resist the Italians no matter what the cost, even if completely surrounded – there could be no question of the French fighting a pitched battle against vastly superior forces. General Orly's battle-plan depended on the employment of every available means to slow down the Italian advance, using artillery, demolition and hit-and-run tactics by small groups of ski troops, so buying time for a gradual withdrawal of the main French forces to a main line of resistance on the axis Mont-Cenis – Termignon – Esseillon.

The French defensive organization in the Beaufortin and Tarentaise areas would be responsible for preventing an Italian breakthrough in the direction of Bourg-Saint-Maurice and Albertville, although the resources available to the French for carrying out this task were slender enough; they comprised only four battalions of fortress troops and forty-four artillery pieces, supported by detachments of ski troops drawn from the 6th and 80th Alpine Fortress Battalions.

French sappers began the work of demolition immediately on the Italian declaration of war, using high explosives to create obstacles in the path of the enemy advance. All civilians in the area were evacuated. Between 10 and 21 June, contact between the opposing forces was limited to skirmishing between ski troops; operating in the difficult atmospheric conditions of high altitude, the French succeeded in dislodging two groups of Italian alpine troops who attempted to establish advance positions at Grand-Cocor and La Galise.

On 21 June, the Italians concentrated their offensive on three principal axes: Petit-Saint-Bernard – Bourg-Saint-Maurice, Col du Mont – Sainte-Foy-Tarentaise, and Col de la Seigne – Les Chapieux. The main thrust came along the latter axis, where the French defences consisted of two companies of the 80th Alpine Fortress Battalion installed on the heights overlooking the Col du Bonhomme and the Col de la Croix-Bonhomme, with two machine-gun sections commanding the Vallée des Glaciers, and two sections of the 80th Alpine Battalion and the 7th Alpine Chasseurs Battalion commanded by Lieutenant Bulle holding the Col d'Enclave. This small force was supported by a battery of 105-mm guns in the Vallée des Contamines, together with two batteries of 75-mm and one of 95-mm near Cormet de Roselend.

Morale among the French alpine troops was excellent, despite the depressing military situation, and every man was determined to do his utmost to stop the Italians in their tracks. Before the Italians could make progress to north or south, they would first have to break the French at the Col d'Enclave and the Col du Bonhomme; they had no way of knowing that bitter French resistance would turn it into a costly undertaking.

Lieutenant Bulle occupied the Col d'Enclave with a single group of Chasseurs on the 20th and decided to set up an observation post on the Tête de Bellaval, a lofty position that offered an unparalleled view of the surrounding terrain. The post was established by noon the following day, Bulle and a small party of skiers making a series of perilous trips in dense fog to deposit weapons and supplies on the peak. As they continued with their task, they heard the noise of gunfire echoing from the mountain walls; it seemed to be coming from the Bellegarde strongpoint, the main French defensive position before the Col d'Enclave, which was held by fifty men under the command of Bulle's friend Sous-Lieutenant Castex. Attacked by a force five times their number, the French put up a spirited resistance, but it was hopeless. Castex was killed, and threequarters of his men were soon casualties.

When the fog lifted in the early afternoon, Bulle saw to his horror that Bellegarde was in Italian hands, and that enemy reinforcements were pouring into the position. From his vantage point, he immediately signalled the French artillery, which opened up a devastating and accurate barrage on the enemy troops milling around on the mountain slopes. A detachment of Italian soldiers tried to advance on Bulle's position, but they were decimated by mortar and machine-gun fire.

The following morning, the Italians attacked in strength. Under heavy fire, Bulle managed to get the following message through to his battalion commander:

My section is in position on the approaches to the Col d'Enclave. The enemy have overwhelmed de Castex and have encircled the Seloges strongpoint [a second defensive position about half a mile from Bellegarde]. In the event of no further orders from you, my section will continue to prevent a passage through the Col d'Enclave. We do not have many men, but we shall hold on. As long as we have a single bullet left, no enemy soldier will break through the Col. Long live eternal France!

Hastily, their fingers numb with cold, the men of Bulle's section scribbled last letters to their families. Bulle placed them in a satchel, together with his message, and handed the bag to one of his chasseurs, Corporal Blanc Ovide. The men watched anxiously as Ovide sped away on his skis, manœuvring skilfully to avoid the enemy bullets that kicked up spurts of snow at his heels, heading down the valley towards the French command post. Then, as the messenger disappeared from sight, Bulle and the others turned to face the enemy and prepared to sell their lives dearly.

The Italians came in a frontal attack, floundering through the snow in a dense wave. Shellfire and machine-gun bullets cut great swathes in their ranks. Blood flowed across the snow, and flocks of chamois, the agile mountain goats, lent an incongruous note to the battle as they bounded across the bodies of dead and dying men, fleeing in terror from the storm of shrapnel that turned their mountain home into a slaughterhouse.

From his observation post, Bulle suddenly spotted a party of Italians attempting to work their way along a ledge below the

F

French position, protected from overhead fire by a rocky out-
crop. Attaching a rope round his waist, the Lieutenant ordered
his men to lower him over the side until he was dangling in
space with a clear view of the infiltrators. Bulle raked the
ledge with his sub-machine-gun, taking the Italians completely
by surprise; only three of them managed to scramble clear,
and they were knocked out by a grenade tossed from above.

Night fell, bringing with it bitter temperatures of twenty
below. Snow, icy wind and hunger were beginning to take their
toll of the French defenders, crouching in holes hacked from
the ice with only tent canvas for protection. There was sporadic firing during the night, but it died away in the early hours,
and at dawn on 23 June a strange calm hung over the em-
battled slopes. Bulle realized that his men, exhausted as they
were, could not remain on the slopes for much longer. The
problem was to get them out of their positions; any movement was likely to attract enemy fire. In the end, Bulle set
out down the mountain alone, making use of the scant available cover, and after an hour of strenuous effort, he rejoined
his adjutant, Sergeant-Major Anxionnaz, at another defensive
position a thousand feet lower down. Surprisingly, he had
drawn no enemy fire at all.

One by one, Bulle's men scrambled down to safety. It was
eight hours before the last chasseur vacated the observation
post. The next morning, under a mantle of fog, Bulle's section
was relieved. It was only when they arrived back at the command post beyond the Col d'Enclave that they learned that an
Armistice had been signed.

On 21 June, meanwhile, the Italians had switched part of
their effort towards Bourg-Saint-Maurice by way of the Petit-
Saint-Bernard pass. Their offensive opened with an air attack
on the town at 06.00, the majority of the bombs falling to the
north of the main street. There were no casualties among the
remaining civilians.

At 08.10, they launched a heavy artillery barrage on the
Redoubt, the French fortress commanding the exit from the
Petit-Saint-Bernard, and pushed fighting patrols forward through

the pass. At 11.20, the French identified the Italian forces engaged in the operation: the Aosta and Val d'Orlo Battalions of the 4th Alpine Infantry Regiment. An hour later, French observers reported a strong enemy column on the Saint-Bernard road; the 75s at once opened up, and their devastating fire halted the Italian advance. At 11.55, the enemy tried again, with the same result.

Shortly after noon, one of the French outposts, situated on the Col du Mont, came under heavy attack. The outpost was held by twenty men of the 3rd Company, 70th Alpine Infantry Battalion. Although outnumbered fifty to one, the detachment, led by Sergeant-Major Bonan, held off the Italians for six hours, withdrawing only when their ammunition was exhausted. The men – one with a broken leg – struggled down the mountainside and rejoined the main body of their unit at Sainte-Foy.

Sporadic artillery fire continued on the Redoubt throughout the afternoon of the 22nd, and although the shells caused little in the way of material damage, they had a telling effect on the nerves of the French garrison as they burst with a deafening roar on the rocks above the Redoubt's bunkers. When the barrage lifted, the Italian infantry attacked, small groups of ten or twelve men dashing across the snow from the cover of one clump of rocks to another. By 16.00, the leading infantry had approached to within a mile of the Redoubt, but they were pinned down by accurate French artillery and small arms fire.

During the night of the 22nd – as black as pitch, with dense fog shrouding the mountains – the French pulled in their outposts to the main defensive area of the Redoubt. By this time all ranks knew that an armistice was being negotiated, but at 23.00, Colonel Morel, commanding the sector, ordered the Redoubt's defenders to continue their resistance until the end of hostilities.

On the morning of the 23rd, the fog cleared, and at 11.00, the Italians, unaware that the French had pulled back, launched a large-scale attack on the abandoned outpost line. The French watched from their main position as the enemy, thrown into some confusion by the unexpected lack of resistance, made a half-hearted attempt to consolidate their newly-gained ground.

Throughout the whole of the following day, both sides sat tight and faced each other; no shots were fired. Finally, in the small hours of 25 June, the French learned that the armistice had been officially signed. At 06.45, two Italian officers approached the Redoubt under a white flag, announced that the war was over and bluntly asked the French commander, Lieutenant Dessertaux, what he intended to do. Dessertaux replied that he had to wait for written orders from his superiors and invited the Italians to have breakfast with him. As the morning went on, more Italian officers arrived, including Colonel Magliani, commanding the 4th Alpine Infantry, and the CO of the ' Aosta ' Battalion which, if it had not been for the armistice, would have led the assault on the Redoubt. There was no animosity between the opposing sides; as time went by, more Frenchmen and Italians began to leave their positions and fraternize in the open.

During the night, the Redoubt's garrison received orders to remain in position while the Armistice Commission determined the strongpoint's future. It was finally evacuated by the French on 3 July and formally handed over to the Italians.

So ended Mussolini's abortive ' Alpine Offensive '. For the French, the bitter taste of their country's defeat was lessened somewhat by the knowledge that in this sector at least, 8,500 of their soldiers had held at bay 52,000 of the enemy's best troops; for the Italians, the failure to penetrate even to their preliminary objectives represented a serious loss of face that would in no way be eradicated by their subsequent military performance in North Africa.

Epilogue

The six weeks between 10 May and 22 June 1940 witnessed one of the fastest and most devastating campaigns in the history of warfare. For the Germans, luck played no small part in the outcome of the campaign; they had taken the new concept of armoured warfare, based on the lightning thrust by tanks with massive air support, and they had employed it intelligently and flexibly – and yet it had been a gamble which, had they encountered sterner resistance coupled with higher qualities of discipline and morale, might not have paid off. What a different story it might have been if more Allied commanders had conducted their counter-attacks with the same dash as the British at Arras, or their defences with the same steadfastness as Franklyn's divisions at Ypres-Comines and de Lattre's 14th Division on the Aisne!

The fact that the Germans achieved so much in so little time was due in no small measure to the incomparable personal leadership of their generals, who conducted their battles at considerable personal risk from command vehicles and spotter aircraft. In the eyes of their British opponents, at least, they earned a respect that was never to desert them, and veterans of the battle looking back over three and a half decades feel unanimously that the German victory was in every way deserved. Yet this 'leadership from in front' had its price; in Erwin Rommel's 7th Panzer Division alone, the 682 men killed during the six-week battle included no fewer than fifty-two officers.

Despite their overall crushing defeat, certain achievements of the Allies during those six weeks should not be forgotten. The Royal Navy and the French Navy were supreme in their

efforts to evacuate Allied forces from the Channel ports, setting a trend for co-operation that was marred only by the
subsequent unhappy destruction of the French Mediterranean
Fleet by the British at Mers-el-Kebir, while between 10 May
and the armistice, the Allied air forces destroyed at least six
hundred enemy aircraft in combat – a fact that placed the
Luftwaffe in no condition to launch an immediate air attack
on the British Isles. It may be no exaggeration to say that the
Battle of Britain was won in the skies of France.

The campaign in Belgium and France brought a new word
to the language of warfare: *Blitzkrieg*, or Lightning War. The
concept of the fast air-supported armoured thrust, however,
remained valid only as long as the supply lines that backed it
up remained unbroken; once those lines were cut, the armoured
spear became brittle and dangerously exposed, as subsequent
events were to prove. The Germans tried *Blitzkrieg* in Russia;
after initial successes, it failed when the logistics system broke
down under the terrible climate and the efforts of Russian
partisans. Rommel tried it in Africa; again he succeeded initially, but then his supply lines were shattered by the Desert
Air Force and by Malta-based bombers that preyed on his
convoys.

From then on, armour became a subordinate part of a mighty
war machine; a machine that achieved victory by pounding
the enemy hard and continually with every weapon in its
arsenal. The day of the swashbuckling armoured dash was gone
for ever – or so it was thought. It took twenty-seven years for
the concept to be resurrected, and it was reborn in what
Rommel and his fellow generals would have applauded as ideal
circumstances from the tactical point of view. In June 1967,
following massive air strikes aimed at neutralizing the enemy
air forces, General Israel Tal's Armoured Brigade swept through
the Sinai desert to the Suez Canal in what was almost a carbon
copy of the German campaign of 1940.

Yet, like that earlier campaign, the Israeli tactics would not
serve again to win a rapid and decisive victory; they could be
used only as long as the attacking armour retained its element

of surprise and as long as the enemy's defences were to some extent unprepared.

Yet, even today, the idea of *Blitzkrieg* is far from dead. In the conduct of a hypothetical conventional war, it forms a major part of the military doctrine of the Warsaw Pact – a power with a potential in air and armour against which the German effort of 1940 pales into insignificance.

Who knows but that in some disastrous future situation, the Battle of France – and indeed of the whole of Western Europe – might not have to be fought again? And who is to say whether the outcome of it would be very different?

Appendix I

ORDER OF BATTLE OF GERMAN LAND FORCES ON
WESTERN FRONT, 9 MAY 1940

Army Group A – von Rundstedt

Fourth Army – von Kluge:
II Korps
V Korps
VIII Korps
XV Panzer Korps
Effective strength: nine infantry divisions and two Panzer
  divisions

Twelfth Army – List:
III Korps
VI Korps
XVIII Korps
Effective strength: ten infantry divisions and one mountain
  division

Sixteenth Army – Busch:
VII Korps
XIII Korps
XXIII Korps
XL Korps (in reserve)
Effective strength: twelve infantry divisions

Armour and Motorized Infantry:
Panzergruppe Kleist
xix Panzer Korps – Guderian: 1st, 2nd and 10th Panzer
    Divisions, ss Grossdeutschland Motorized Regiment
xli Panzer Korps – Reinhardt: 6th and 8th Panzer Divisions
xiv Korps – von Wietersheim: 2nd, 3rd and 29th Motorized
    Divisions.

Army Group Reserve:
ii Korps (three infantry divisions)

Army Group B – von Bock

Eighteenth Army – Küchler:
x Korps
xxvi Korps
Effective strength: one airborne division (the 22nd), two motor-
    ized ss divisions, one cavalry division, one armoured
    division (9th Panzer), four infantry divisions

Sixth Army – von Reichenau:
iv Korps
ix Korps
xi Korps
xxvii Korps
xvi Panzer Korps
Effective strength: fourteen infantry and two Panzer divisions

Army Group Reserve: One Korps with five infantry divisions,
    one motorized infantry division, and one ss motorized
    division

Army Group C – von Leeb

First Army – Witzleben:
Four Korps with eleven infantry divisions.
    G

Seventh Army – Dollman:
Two Korps with four infantry divisions

Army Group Reserve: four infantry divisions

GHQ *Reserve*

Second Army – Weichs
Ninth Army – Blaskowitz
Effective strength: six Korps and two 'skeleton' Korps with a
   total of 41 infantry divisions

Total German land forces assigned to 'Plan Yellow' on 10 May:
114 infantry divisions
Ten armoured divisions
Four motorized divisions
Two SS motorized divisions
One cavalry division
One airborne division

Appendix 2

ORDER OF BATTLE OF FRENCH ARMY GROUP ONE
(NORTH-EAST), 10 MAY 1940

First Army – General J. G. M. Blanchard

III Corps – General de la Laurencie:
1st Motorized Division
2nd North African Division

IV Corps – General Aymes:
15th Motorized Division
Moroccan Infantry Division

V Corps – General Altmayer:
12th Motorized Division
5th North African Division

Cavalry Corps – General Prioux:
2nd Light Armoured Division
3rd Light Armoured Division

Second Army – General C. L. C. Huntziger

X Corps – General Grandsard:
3rd North African Division
55th Infantry Division

XVIII Corps – General Doyen:
1st Colonial Infantry Division
41st Infantry Division

Armour:
2nd Cavalry Division
5th Cavalry Division
1st Cavalry Brigade

Ninth Army – General A. G. Corap

II Corps – General Bouffet:
5th Motorized Division

XI Corps – General Martin:
18th Infantry Division
22nd Infantry Division

XLI Corps – General Libaud:
61st Infantry Division
102nd Fortress Division

Armour:
1st Cavalry Division
4th Cavalry Division

Army Reserve:
4th North African Division
53rd Infantry Division

Seventh Army (AG One reserve army up to May 1940 – General
    Giraud)

I Corps – General Sciard:
25th Motorized Division

38th Infantry Division
4th Division Reconnaissance Group (attached)
21st Division Reconnaissance Group (attached)

xvi Corps – General Fagalde:
9th Motorized Division
60th Infantry Division
68th Division

In reserve:
4th Division
21st Division

Armour:
1st Light Armoured Division

Appendix 3

ORDER OF BATTLE OF THE BRITISH EXPEDITION-
ARY FORCE, 10 MAY 1940

Commander-in-Chief: General the Viscount Gort, vc

1 *Corps* – Lieutenant-General M. G. H. Barker

1st Division – Major General Alexander:
1st Guards Brigade
2nd Brigade
3rd Brigade

2nd Division – Major General Loyd:
4th Brigade
5th Brigade
6th Brigade

48th (South Midland) Division – Major General Thorne:
143rd Brigade
144th Brigade
145th Brigade

11 *Corps* – A. F. Brooke

3rd Division – Major General Montgomery:
7th Guards Brigade

8th Brigade
9th Brigade

4th Division – Major General Johnson:
10th Brigade
11th Brigade
12th Brigade

50th (Northumbrian) Division – Major General Martel:
150th Brigade
151st Brigade
25th Brigade

III *Corps* – Lieutenant General Sir Ronald Adam

42nd (East Lancashire) Division – Major General Holmes:
125th Brigade
126th Brigade
127th Brigade

44th (Home Counties) Division – Major General Osborne:
131st Brigade
132nd Brigade
133rd Brigade

GHQ *Reserve*

5th Division – Major General Franklyn:
13th Brigade
17th Brigade

Added to BEF *after 10 May*

23rd (Northumbrian) Division – Major General Herbert:
69th Brigade
70th Brigade

46th (North Midland and West Riding) Division – Major General Curtis:
137th Brigade
138th Brigade
139th Brigade

Engaged in Somme area

12th (Eastern) Division – Major General Petre:
35th Brigade
36th Brigade
37th Brigade

In Maginot Line (10 May) and with French Tenth Army (1 June)

51st (Highland) Division – Major General Fortune:
152nd Brigade
153rd Brigade
154th Brigade

Royal Artillery

Total artillery units supporting BEF: 37 field regiments, 11 medium regiments, 16 anti-aircraft regiments, 11 anti-tank regiments.

Royal Armoured Corps

12th Royal Lancers (armoured cars)
Divisional Cavalry (4th/7th Royal Dragoon Guards, 5th Royal Inniskilling Dragoon Guards, 13th/18th Royal Hussars, 15th/19th King's Royal Hussars)

1st Light Armoured Reconnaissance Brigade
1st Army Tank Brigade

Note: the 1st Armoured Division began to arrive in France on 20 May and was in action south of the Somme.

Disposition of Anglo - French armies on 9 May 1940.

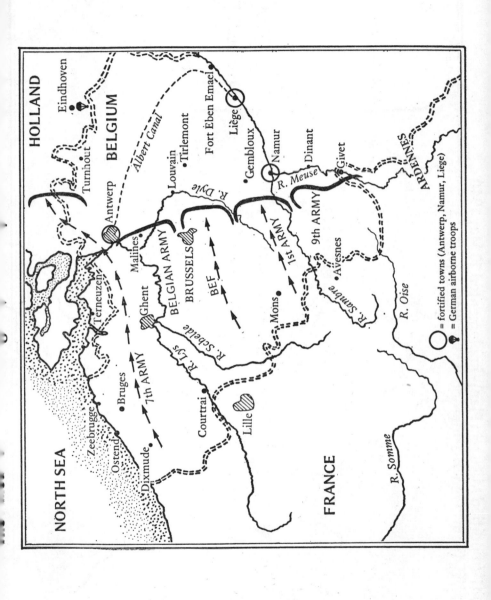

'Sichelschnitt' (modified Manstein Plan) – implemented 10 May 1940

Encirclement of the northern armies

GREAT BRITAIN

Dover

ENGLISH CHANNEL

Dieppe

FRANCE

Abbeville

Nouvion

Boulogne

Calais

Dunkirk

Ostend

Bruges

Ghent

Antwerp

R. Schelde

R. Dyle

BRUSSELS

BELGIUM

Namur

R. Meuse

R. Sambre

Vervins

Guise

St Quentin

R. Oise

R. Somme

Amiens

Puisieux

Doullens

Hesdin

St Omer

Merville

PANZERS HALT 22 MAY

Armentières

Courtrai

R. Lys

Lille

Douai

Arras

BRITISH COUNTER ATTACK 21 MAY

Cambrai

Le Câteau

1st PANZER KORPS

10th PANZER KORPS

2nd PANZER KORPS

GUDERIAN

REINHARDT

HOTH

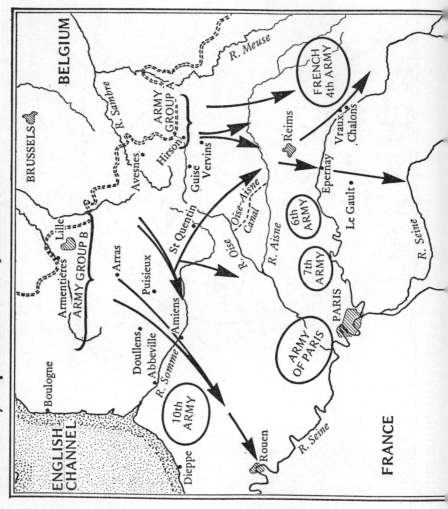

German breakthrough on the Somme and Aisne and French army dispositions on 12 June 1940

Bibliography

Bauer, E., *Der Panzerkrieg* (Bonn, 1965)

Bekker, Cajus, *The Luftwaffe War Diaries* (London, 1965)

Benoist-Mechin, J., *Sixty Days That Shook the West* (London, 1956)

Bryant, Arthur, *The Turn of the Tide* (London, 1957)

Churchill, W. S., *The Second World War*, vols 1 and 2 (London, 1948–9)

Clark, Douglas, *Three Days to Catastrophe* (London, 1966)

Draper, Theodore, *The Six Weeks' War* (London, 1946)

Ellis, Major L. F., *The War in France and Flanders, 1939-40* (London, 1953)

Fuller, Major General J. F. C., *Decisive Battles of the Western World* (London, 1956)

Galland, Adolf, *The First and the Last* (London, 1954)

de Gaulle, General Charles, *War Memoirs*, vol. 1 (London, 1955)

Goutard, Col. A., *The Battle of France, 1940* (London, 1958)

Guderian, General Heinz, *Panzer Leader* (London, 1952)

Habe, Hans, *A Thousand Shall Fall* (London, 1942)

Halder, Franz, *Kriegstagebuch*, 3 vols (Stuttgart, 1962–4)

Horne, Alistair, *To Lose a Battle* (London, 1969)

Ironside, General Sir Edmund, *The Ironside Diaries* (London, 1962)

Jackson, Robert, *Before the Storm:* RAF *Bomber Command, 1939–42* (London, 1972)

Jacobsen, H. A., *Decisive Battles of World War* II (London, 1965)

Liddell Hart, B. H., *The Other Side of the Hill* (London, 1948)

Liddell Hart, B. H., *The Tanks, 1939–45* (London, 1959)

Manstein, Field Marshal F. E. von, *Lost Victories* (London, 1958)

Mellenthin, Major General F. W. von, *Panzer Battles, 1939–45* (London, 1955)

Mengin, Robert, *No Laurels for de Gaulle* (London, 1967)

Rommel, Field Marshal E., *The Rommel Papers*, ed. Liddell Hart (London, 1951)

Rowe, Vivian, *The Great Wall of France* (New York, 1959)

Shirer, William L., *The Rise and Fall of the Third Reich* (London, 1962)

Spears, E. L., *Assignment to Catastrophe* (London, 1954)

Taylor, A. J. P., *Origins of the Second World War* (London, 1961)

Thompson, Laurence, *1940* (London, 1966)

Westphal, General S., *The German Army in the West* (London, 1951)

Weygand, General Maxime, *Recalled to Service* (London, 1952)

Wilmot, Chester, *The Struggle for Europe* (London, 1952)

Index

AFVS tanks, 13, 67, 85, 95, 135
Aa canal, 132
Aachen, 41, 43
Abbeville, 35, 105, 106, 135, 138
Adair, Lieutenant-Colonel Alan, 125
Adinkirk, 127
Adinkerne-Dunkirk road, 130
Advanced Air Striking Force, 37, 51, 79, 80, 113, 140
Africa, 156; see also North Africa
Ailette River, 104, 136
Air Component, BEF, 22
Aisne River, 64, 88, 91, 92, 93, 94, 104, 105, 135, 136, 137, 142, 143, 146, 155
Albania, 17
Albert, 105
Albert Canal, 40, 41, 42, 49, 52
Albertville, 149
Alconbury, Huntingdonshire, (RAF), 55
Algerian Infantry, 25
Allied Intelligence, 26, 37
Allied Supreme Council, 26
Allies, 27, 29, 35, 72, 155-6
Alpes-Maritime, 28, 148
Alps, 28, 148
Altmayer, General René, 50, 110, 111, 112, 113, 121
Altstadt, 60
Altvatar, 42
Amiens, 27, 34, 38, 105, 106, 107, 136, 140, 142
Amiot (bomber), 16, 36, 79, 143
Amsterdam, 53

Anchamps, 76
Andalsnes, 38
Anglo-French Expeditionary Force, 38; see also BEF
Anhée, 66, 82
Anschluss, 3
Anseremme, 67
Antwerp, 26, 27, 50, 61, 62, 63, 100
Anxoinnax, Sergeant Major, 152
Ardenne, 48, 49
Ardenne Canal, 86, 87, 90
Ardennes, the, 26, 27, 28, 29, 33, 34, 46, 51, 64, 65, 72, 76, 98
Armée de l'Air, 15, 25, 36, 37, 51, 52, 137, 140
armour in Second World War, 13
Arnhem, 57
Arras, 38, 99, 102, 109, 111, 112, 113, 116, 117, 118, 120, 121, 132, 155
Assault Group Koch, 41, 42
Athies, 110
Attichy, 142
Attigny, 142
Austria, annexation of, 1938, 2, 3
Autoroute, 28, 141
Avesnes, 96, 97

B tanks, 35, 83, 85, 90, 103, 104, 143
B.1 tanks, 13, 24, 82, 83, 84, 85, 89, 90
Bad Zwischenahn, 57

Balan, 72
Balck, Colonel, 74
Balkans, 18
Bar, River, 76, 86, 89, 142
Barratt, Air Marshal, 50, 51, 72, 79
Basle, 20
Bastogne, 46
Battles (airplanes), see Fairey
Bavai, 101
Bazeilles, 72
Beauchesne, General, 61
Beaufortin, 149
Beauvais-Dieppe road, 140
Beck, General Josef, 5, 9
Belgian Air Force, 47, 50
Belgian Army, 27, 49, 62, 68, 107, 122, 126; mobilization of, 32; High Command, 32; units: Cavalry Corps, 48; 2nd Cavalry Division, 67; 7th Division, 47; 14th Division, 48; 7th Infantry Regiment, (at Eben Emael), 40, 44
Belgium, 31, 32, 34, 38, 41, 52, 65, 66, 77, 80, 98, 101, 121, 122, 156; and occupation of Rhineland, 2; neutrality of, 19, 22; and Maginot line, 20; expected German attack, 26, 27, 28, 29; and 'Sichelschnitt', 33, 34; German invasion, 41-52
Bellegarde, 150, 151
Belval, 143
Berchtesgaden talks, 6
Bergen-op-Zoom, 53, 61, 62
Bergues, 126
Bergues-Furnes canal, 129
Berlaimont, 101
Berlin, 8, 9, 10, 11, 32
Bernaville, 68
Berthonnal Farm, 120
Besson, General Antoine, 28, 138
Béziers de la Fosse, General, 98
Billotte, General Gaston-Henri-Gustave, 27, 28, 32, 48, 49, 62, 69, 79, 91, 101, 111, 112, 114, 121

Bioul, 68
Bismarck, Colonel von, 69
Bitburg, 46
Blanchard, General, 97, 121
Blangy, 138
Blenheims, 51, 55, 79, 80; IVFS, see also RAF squadrons
Blies, River, 25, 26
Blitzkrieg, 156-7
Bloch 210s (bomber), 16, 36; 151, 36
Blomberg, Field Marshal Werner von, 3
Boch, General Feodor von, 29, 33, 35, 45, 100, 138
Bohemia, 12, 16
Bois de la Marfée, 88; see also Marfée Wood
bomber aircraft, 15
Bomber Command, see RAF
Bonan, Sergeant Major, 153
Boncourt, 103
Bonnet, Georges, 6, 18
Booth, Second Lieutenant, 128, 131
Bordeaux, 145
Bouchain, 102
Boucher, General, 70
Bouffet, General, 82, 95
Bouillon, 34
Boulogne, 133, 134
Bourg-Saint-Maurice, 149, 152
Bouvellemont, 94
Bouvignes, 69
Brandenburgers, 56-7; see also German army
Brauchitsch, General Walther von, 29, 32
Bray Dunes, 130
Breda, 27, 61, 62
Breguet 693 (bombers), 36, 52, 140
Breskens, 61
Bresle River, 138
Bristol Blenheims, 37
Britain, at Munich, 2; and occupation of Rhineland, 2; and invasion of Czechoslovakia, 4,

5, 6, 7, 8, 9, 16; and Poland, 17, 22; declares war on Germany, 23; and Nazi-Soviet Non-Aggression Pact, 18

British Air Force: *see* Royal Air Force

British Air Forces in France, 50, 72, 79

British Army, 134; military strength, 19; armour of, 35; early days of War, 38; GHQ, 107; air component, 37

British Army Units:

Corps
 I, 27, 107, 109, 123, 128
 II, 27, 107, 122, 144

Divisions
 1st, 107, 108, 124, 127
 1st Armoured, 134-5, 138
 1st Canadian, 138, 144
 1st Infantry, 124
 2nd, 107, 108
 3rd, 107, 125, 126, 127
 4th Infantry, 107, 108, 110, 124, 125
 5th, 27, 107, 108, 110, 120, 121, 122, 123, 126, 127
 12th, 110
 23rd Infantry, 110
 42nd Infantry, 107, 126, 127
 42nd Territorials, 27
 44th Territorials, 27
 46th Infantry, 107, 127
 48th Territorials, 27, 107, 108
 50th Northumbrians, 38
 50th Territorials, 27, 107, 110, 118, 120, 121, 122, 123, 124, 125, 126, 127
 51st Highland, 27, 138, 141
 52nd Lowland, 138, 144

Brigades
 British Army Tank, 35
 Rifle, 134
 1st Army Tank, 111, 112, 120, 133
 2nd, 135
 10th, 125
 11th, 125

13th Infantry, 108, 109, 111, 112, 116, 117, 118, 119, 120, 122, 123, 124, 126
17th Infantry, 108, 112, 117, 118, 119, 122, 123
35th, 105
143rd, 122, 123
150th Infantry, 38, 112, 118, 120, 121, 124, 126, 127, 134
151st Infantry, 112, 117, 120
153rd, 138
154th, 138
157th, 144

Regiments
 2nd Cameronians, 118, 123
 Duke of Wellingtons, 129
 East Yorkshire, 38
 9th Field, 118
 91st Field, 118
 97th Field, 118
 Green Howards, 111, 127
 3rd Grenadier Guards, 124, 125
 10th Hussars, 135
 13/18th Hussars, 124, 125
 2nd North Staffords, 124, 125
 2nd Northamptons, 108, 119, 123, 124
 Northumberland Fusiliers 127-8, 129
 Queen's Bays, 135
 Royal Engineers, 124, 125
 2nd Royal Scots Fusiliers, 123, 124
 Royal Sussex, 105
 Royal Tank, 111, 134, 135
 7th Royal Warwickshire, 123
 6th Seaforth Highlanders, 123
 2nd Sherwood Foresters, 124
 South Staffordshire, 129
 1st Welsh Guards, 109
 2nd Wiltshire, 118, 123, 124

Battalions
 6th Black Watch, 124-5
 4th East Yorkshires, 38
 4th Green Howards, 38, 127
 5th Green Howards, 38
 Guards, 124
 2nd Royal Inniskilling Fusiliers,

108, 109, 118, 119, 123
British Expeditionary Force,
  (BEF), 22, 27, 41, 49, 62, 80,
  98, 107-35, 144
British Fleet, 8, 15, 155
Brocard, General, 87, 89, 90
Brooke, General Sir Alan, 27,
  122, 124, 144
Bruché, General, 94, 95
Bruneau, General, 83, 84, 85
Brussels, 33
Brustheim, 50
Bruyère, 103
Buché, General, 96
Buisson, General, 90
Bulle, Lieutenant, 150, 151, 152
Bulson, 75, 87
Busch, General Ernst von, 33,
  35
Bush, Lieutenant-Colonel, 127
Butler, Major, 109
Butterworth, Lieutenant-
  Colonel, 125
Butzweilerhof, 41

Calais, 133, 134
Cambrai, 95, 99, 109
Camps-en-Amiennois, 108
Canal du Nord, 102
Carter, Ken, 38
'Case Green' ('Fall Grun'), 3,
  5
'Case Yellow' ('Fall Gelb'), 28
Castex, Sous-Lieutenant, 150,
  151
Câteau, le, 97
Câtelet, le, 98
Cauchie, Sergeant, 127
Chabreleix, 67
Chagny, 93
Chalons-sur-Marne, 143
Chamberlain, Neville, 6, 7;
  meetings with Hitler, 6, 7;
  negotiations with Germany, 8,
  9, 10, 11; and Poland, 22
Channel, English, 34, 105
Chanoine, General, 86, 90, 93
Charleroi, 50, 80, 94, 98

Charleville, 99, 132
chasseurs-éclaireurs, reconnais-
  sance troops, 28
Château-Porcien, 92, 93, 142
Château Regnault, 77
Chauny, 72
Chéhéry, 75
Chemery, 87
Cherbourg, 38, 141, 144, 145
Chiers, River, 71, 72
Churchill, Brigadier, 117
Churchill, Winston, speech on
  Munich, 11; evacuation of BEF,
  134, 144
Clairfayts, 97
Cojeul, River, 112
Col du Bonhomme, 150
Col de la Croix-Bonhomme, 150
Col d'Enclave, 150, 151, 152
Col du Mont, 149-50, 153
Col de la Seigne, 150
Cologne, 1, 30, 41, 43, 44
Comblain-au-Pont, 48
Comines, 123, 124, 125
Compiègne, 95, 143, 146
'concrete' Assault Detachment,
  42-3, 45
Condé, 26
Connage, 75
Cooke-Collis, Major, 129, 131
Corap, General André-Georges,
  27, 69, 70, 71, 95
Corbie, 105
Cormet de Roselend, 150
Crehen, 52
Crozat Canal, 102, 105
Curignan, 74
Curtiss Hawk 75s, 36
Czechoslovakia, 2, 3, 11, 12, 16,
  42; Sudeten Germans in, 4, 5,
  6, 7; negotiations with Hitler,
  10

D.I tanks, 13
D.2 tanks, 13, 103
DFS 230 heavy assault gliders,
  40-4
Daladier, Edouard, 6, 9, 10

Danzig, 18
Dauphiné, 28, 148
Deckendorf, 46
de Gaulle, Charles, 13, 81, 103, 104, 105, 135
de Lattre de Tassigny, General Jean, 93, 142, 155
de la Vigerie, General d'Astier, 51, 72
Delft, 55
Delmenhorst, 52
Dempsey, Brigadier (later General Sir Miles), 119, 124, 126
Denain, 101
Dendre River, 109, 110
Deslaurens, Colonel, 61, 63
Dessertaux, Lieutenant, 154
Dewoitine D.520, 36
Dickebusch, 128
Dieppe, 140, 141
Dijon, 47, 92, 145
Dinant, 33, 65, 67, 69, 70, 71, 73, 79, 81, 83
Dirschau, 23
Dom-le-Mesnil, 76, 87
Donchéry, 74, 76, 86, 87
Dordrecht, 56, 57, 58
Dornier 17s, 73
Douai, 120, 121
Douglas DB-7 bomber, 16, 140
Driessen, 61
Dubuy, 48
Dunkirk, 61, 122, 128, 131, 132, 133
Durand, General, 61
Duren, 43
Dusseldorf, 39
Dutch army, eight divisions of, 27; mobilized, 32; Infantry regiment, 61; Queen's regiment, 53; *see also* Netherlands Army Aviation
Dyle line, 48, 49, 107
Dyle Plan, 26, 27
Dyle River, 26

Eben Emael, 40, 41, 42, 43, 44, 47

Ecurie, 119
Elbeuf, 140
Englefontaine, 101
Ennemane, 75
Ermeton-sur-Biert, 85
Erpion, 83
Escaut Plan, 26, 48
Escaut River, 26, 101, 102, 109
Esch-sur-Alzette, 46
Esseillon, 149
Etreux, 94
Eu, 138
Evreux, 144

FCMS tanks, 21
Fabry, Colonel, 14
Fagalde, General, 27, 62
Fairey Battles, 37, 50, 51, 79, 140
Fairey Fox, 50
'Fall Gelb' (Case Yellow), 28, 29, 30, 31
'Fall Grun' (Case Green), 3, 5
'Fall Rot' (Case Red), 136
Fassberg, 52
Felmy, General Hellmuth, 32
Fenwick, PSM, 128
Ferrand, Edmond, 145
Fiat CR 42s, 50
Ficheux, 115
Fieseler Storch, 45
fighter aircraft, 15
Fismes, 105
Flavigny, General, 88, 89, 90, 142
Flavion, 67, 82
Fleurus, 50
Flushing, 61, 63
Foch, Marshal, 146
Fokker D 21s, 53; TVs, CXs, CVs, 54; CSs, 55
Foreign Legion, 24
Fôret de Mormal, 48, 100, 102
Forges-les-Eaux, 140
Fort Donaumont, 40
Fort Pepinster, 52
Fortune, General, 138, 141
Fosse, 95

France, 156; alliance with
Poland, 17, 19, 22; Maginot
line, 20, 21; declares war on
Germany, 23; German attack
on airbases, 47; at Munich, 2;
invasion of Czechoslovakia, 4,
5, 6, 7, 8, 9, 10; machine tool
industry of, 14; Third Republic,
14; aircraft industry of, 15;
bomber production, 16
'Frankforce', 120
Franklyn, Major-General H. E.,
27, 110, 111, 117, 118, 119,
120, 121, 122, 123, 124, 125,
126, 129, 155
Freiburg-im-Breisgau, 47
French Air Force, 15 see also
Armée de l'Air
French Army, gaps in tactical
structure, 2, 3; attempts to
modernize, 12, 13; armoured
divisions, 13, 24, 35; numerical
superiority of, 22; on N.E.
frontier, 23; and 'Fall Gelb',
32; and Dyle Plan, 41
French Army Units:
Groups:
  1, 27, 28, 32, 62, 79
  2, 25, 28
  3, 28, 138
  4, 142, 143
Armies:
  First, 27, 48, 80, 92, 96, 98,
    101, 102, 106, 107, 133
  Second, 27, 28, 66, 67, 70, 71,
    73, 76, 81, 86, 88, 89, 90, 91,
    93, 136, 142, 143
  Third, 25, 26, 28, 136, 138, 142
  Fourth, 25, 26, 28, 142, 143
  Fifth, 25, 26, 28
  Sixth (Army of the Alps), 28,
    94, 102, 121, 136, 142, 148-54
  Seventh, 27, 57, 61, 62, 63, 136,
    143, 144
  Ninth, 27, 48, 65, 67, 69, 70,
    71, 76, 82-3, 86, 90, 94, 95,
    97, 98, 102
  Tenth, 134, 136, 140, 141, 144

Armée de Paris, 144
Corps:
  Armoured Corps, 111, 112
  Cavalry 47, 48, 49, 80, 111
  I, 105
  II, 52, 65, 67, 92, 95
  III, 49, 103
  IV, 49, 103
  V, 25, 48, 49, 50, 102, 111, 121
  VIII, 102
  X, 70, 72, 73, 74, 76, 93
  XI, 65, 66, 81, 82, 83, 141
  XIV, 28
  XV, 28, 71
  XVI, 28
  XVIII, 71, 72
  XXI, 88, 89, 142
  XLI, 71, 76, 92, 93
Divisions:
  1st Armoured, 80, 82, 83, 84,
    85, 96
  1st Cavalry, 65, 67, 82, 84
  1st Colonial, 89
  1st Light Armoured, 61
  1st Light Mechanized, 118
  1st Motorized, 49
  1st North African, 93
  2nd Armoured, 80, 92, 94, 95,
    105
  2nd Cavalry, 89, 134, 135, 138
  2nd Chasseurs Ardennais, 49,
    66
  2nd Colonial, 28
  2nd Light Armoured, 48, 101
  2nd North African, 49
  3rd Armoured, 48, 81, 87, 88,
    140
  3rd Light, 105
  3rd Motorized, 88, 89, 90
  3rd North African, 70
  4th Armoured, 103, 104, 105,
    135
  4th Cavalry, 48, 65, 67
  4th Infantry, 102
  4th North African, 61, 62, 82,
    84, 96
  5th Cavalry, 86, 87, 134, 135,
    138

5th Colonial, 138; 5th Moroccan, 49, 96
5th Motorized, 65, 71, 96
5th North African, 48, 49, 101
8th Cuirassiers, 48
9th, 61, 62
9th Motorized, 62
11th 'Iron' Division, 25, 143
12th Cuirassiers, 48
12th Motorized, 49
14th, 86, 92, 155
18th Infantry, 65, 66, 67, 69, 70, 82, 83, 92, 96
21st, 61, 62
22nd, 66, 70, 82, 83, 91, 92, 96
23rd, 105
25th Motorized, 61, 62
28th Infantry, 104
31st Alpine, 138, 141
36th Infantry, 93
41st, 71
43rd, 81, 101
44th, 93
53rd, 93
53rd Infantry, 87
55th Infantry, 70, 71, 75, 76, 86, 87
60th, 61, 63
61st Infantry, 70, 77, 78, 82, 83, 90, 91, 92
64th (mountain), 148
65th (mountain), 148
66th, 148
68th, 61, 63
71st Infantry, 70, 75, 86
72nd Artillery, 139
77th Infantry, 84
87th, 93
101 Fortress, 101
102 Fortress, 77, 86, 87
Brigades:
  Alpine Fortress Demi-Brigades, 148
  1st Cavalry, 86, 87, 92, 93
  3rd Spahis, 93
  6th Armoured, 103
  8th Armoured, 103
  42nd Malgache, 77, 91

52nd, 90, 91
Regiments:
  Sengalese, 138
  1st Ardennais, 46
  2nd Cuirassiers, 52
  2nd Algerian, 65, 66
  2nd Moroccan, 65, 66
  3rd Cuirassiers, 104
  5th Machine Gun, 46
  6th Cuirassiers, 61
  7th Motorized Dragoons, 104
  8th Infantry, 81
  10th Cuirassiers, 104
  14th Motorized Dragoons, 81
  19th, 66, 84
  22nd Colonial Infantry, 135
  39th Infantry, 65, 68, 69, 70, 96
  62nd, 66, 96
  66th, 65, 66, 69
  77th, 65, 66, 69
  84th Fortress Infantry, 96-7
  116th, 96
  119th, 66
  125th, 96
  129th Infantry, 67, 68, 81
  148th, 87
  152nd Infantry, 93, 94
  158th, 101
  208th Infantry, 94
  213th Infantry, 75
  224th, 61
  239th Infantry, 87
  248th Infantry, 78
  318th Artillery, 66
  322nd Artillery, 103
  331st Infantry, 76, 86
Battalions:
  1st of 52nd Demi-Brigade, 91
  2nd of 52nd Demi-Brigade, 91
  2nd Dismounted Dragoons, 103, 138
  2nd Malagache, 77, 91
  2nd, 103
  3rd Moroccans, 101
  4th Chasseurs, 135
  5th Chasseurs à Pieds, 83, 84, 85

6th Alpine Fortress, 149
7th Tank, 75
8th Chasseurs, 93
10th Chasseurs, 102
10th Cuirassiers, 135
11th Dismounted Dragoons, 52
14th Dragoons, 68
16th Chasseurs à Pieds, 88
24th, 103
25th Algerian Tirailleurs, 82
25th Hotchkiss, 83, 85, 97
26th Hotchkiss, 83, 85
27th B.I, 85
28th B.I, 82, 84, 85
37th B.I, 82, 85
41st B.I, 87
42nd Hotchkiss, 87
45th Hotchkiss, 87, 88
49th B.I, 87, 88
67th Cavalry, 89
70th Alpine Infantry, 153
80th, 149, 150
reserve of 129th Infantry regiment, 68
French Government; and occupation of Rhineland, 2, 3; and invasion of Czechoslovakia, 6, 7; and Nazi-Soviet Non-Aggression Pact, 18; and Nazi occupation of Paris, 146-7
French High Command, 26, 27, 28
French Intelligence, 12, 13
French National Assembly, 20
French Navy, 63, 155
Frère, General Aubert, 102, 105, 121
Fresnes, 118
Frisian Islands, 52
Führer, the, see Hitler, Adolf
Furnes, 126
Fürst, Colonel, 68

Gamelin, General Maurice, 25, 27, 62, 72, 107
Garde Republique, 24
Garland, Flying Officer, 51
Gaudin, Charles, 145

Gaulier, 74, 75, 79
Gembloux, 49
Gembloux Gap, 49, 80
Gennep, 57
Georges, General Alphonse, 26, 80, 89, 121
German Air Force : see Luftwaffe
German army : General Staff, 5, 28, 29; formation of Panzers, 13, 19; Panzer tactics, 22; Panzer training, 32; and invasion of Low Countries, 46, 47, 49, 60, 61; in France, 70, 132, 133; operation NIWI, 46; military intelligence, 56
German Army Units :
Groups
A, 29, 33, 35, 36, 136
B, 29, 33, 35, 36, 99, 136
C, 33, 34, 36
Armies
First, 33
Fourth, 33, 66, 96, 145
Sixth, 33, 57, 80, 123
Seventh, 33
Twelfth, 33, 99, 100
Sixteenth, 33, 35
Eighteenth, 33, 59, 80, 144
Corps
II, 66
V, 66
VIII, 66
XIV, Motorized, 33, 95, 99
XV, Armoured, 33, 66, 73, 136, 138
XVI, Armoured, 47, 49, 52, 99, 100
XIX, Armoured, 29, 33, 70, 73, 75, 94, 95, 98, 99
XXI, 73
XXXVIII, 141
XXXIX, 85, 136, 140, 143
Divisions – Panzer
1st Panzer, 23, 33, 46, 47, 71, 73, 74, 75, 76, 87, 89, 93, 98, 105, 106, 143
2nd, 33, 71, 74, 75, 76, 87, 93, 98, 105, 106

3rd, 47, 99
4th, 23, 47, 99, 133
5th, 33, 66, 67, 68, 84, 99, 133, 141; (armoured)
6th, 33, 71, 77, 98
7th, 33, 66, 67, 68, 69, 79, 81, 82, 83, 84, 95, 99, 110, 114, 115, 116, 133, 139, 141
8th, 33, 71, 77, 91
9th, 56, 57, 58, 62, 134
10th, 33, 71, 74, 76, 98, 104, 106
Divisions – Others
2nd Motorized, 141
8th Infantry, 145
18th, 125, 126
20th Motorized, 99
29th Motorized, 89, 104
31st, 126
61st, 126
87th Infantry, 144
ss Totenkopf Motorized, 114, 116
Regiments
Flak, 33, 95
ss Grossdeutschland, 33, 46, 74, 76, 89
1st Fallschirmjager, 53
1st Panzer Rifles, 74
5th Panzer Anti-Tank, 84
6th Rifles, 114-15
7th Rifles, 115
16th Infantry, 57
25th Panzer, 84, 110
31st Panzer, 84
Battalions
3rd Grossdeutschland, 46
3rd Fallschirmjager, 53
Commando Units
Brandenburgers, 56
German High Command, 29, 32, 39, 99, 100
German Government, 18
Germany, proposed offensive in West, 2; at Munich, 2; invasion of Czechoslovakia, 2, 3, 6, 8, 9, 12, 16; machine tools industry, 14; military aircraft, 15; mili-

tary strength, 19; Britain and France declare war on, 23
Ghent, 26
Ghyvelde, 130, 131
Giraud, General Henri, 27, 57, 62, 95, 97, 98
Givet, 64, 65
Gloster Gladiators, 37, 50
Godesberg, 7, 8
Goebbels, Dr Joseph, 5
Goellnicht, Second Lieutenant, 129
Göring, Hermann, 132
Gort, General Lord, 27, 109, 110, 112, 113, 114, 120, 121, 122, 126
Grand-Cocor, 149
'Granite' Assault Detachment, 42-3
Gravelines, 126
Gray, Flight Sergeant, 51
Gray-sur-Saône, 145
Greece, 17
Groupe de Chasse Polonaise, 24
Guderian, General Heinz, 13, 33, 34-5, 46, 70, 71, 75, 79, 92, 93, 94, 98, 99, 103, 104, 106, 115, 132, 133, 142, 143, 145
Gutersloh, 43, 44, 52

Hague, The, 52, 55, 56, 59
Hal, 108, 109
Halder, General Franz, 5, 9, 29, 32
Halen, 48
'Halt Befehl', 132, 133, 134
Ham, 102, 105
Hangest, 138
Hannu, 52
Hartlieb, General Max von, 66, 141
Hasselt, 48
Hastière, 66, 67
Haut-le-Wastia, 81
Haute-Marne, 64
Haydon, Brigadier, 131
Hedderich, Lieutenant, 46
Heinkel 111s 45, 47, 52, 53, 59,

60, 73; HE 59s, 57, 58
Henschel 123s, 45, 95
Hernicourt, 108
Hildesheim, 41
Hirson, 94
Hitler, Adolf, 2, 99; and invasion of Czechoslovakia, 2, 3, 4, 5, 6, 7, 8, 9, 10, 11, 12, 16; and *Anschluss*, 3; and 'Halt Befehl', 132, 133; and occupation of France, 146; meetings with Chamberlain, 6, 7; and '*Fall Gelb*', 29, 30; and 'Sichelschnitt', 33, 34
Hocke, Lieutenant, 56
Hoeppner, General, Erich, 47, 52
Hohne, Lieutenant-Colonel, 60
Holland, 38, 41, 47, 65, 80; neutrality of, 19; and Dyle Plan, 26-7; and '*Fall Gelb*', 29; and 'Sichelschnitt', 33; and German Invasion, 41, 52-63; Hollandisch Diep, 64
Hollebeke, 122, 124
Hönmanns, Major Erich, 1, 30, 31, 32
Hotchkiss tanks, 24, 52, 69, 75, 83, 90, 103, 143; H.35s, 13
Hoth, General Hermann, 33, 66, 73, 99, 136, 138
Hotton, 67
Houtham, 123, 124, 129
Houx, 67, 68, 69, 73, 81
Hubicki, Major-General, 58, 134
Hungarians, in Czechoslovakia, 4
Huntziger, General Charles, 27, 69, 70, 71, 86, 87, 89, 142, 146
Hurricanes, 37
Huy, 48

Ihler, General, 141
'Iron' Assault Detachment, 42-3, 45
Isenburghe, 129
Italian armies, 148-54
Italian fighter strength, 15

Italy, 9, 10, 11, 17; against the French in the Alps, 28, 146, 148-54

Joffre, Marshal Joseph Cesar, 19
Juin, General, 49
Juneville, 143
Junkers: 87 divebombers, 23, 37, 45, 57, 73; 52 transports, 41, 42, 43, 44, 53, 54, 55, 57

Kampfgeschwader: KG 2, 73; KG 3, 73; KG 4, 52, 53; KG 53, 73; KG 54, 59, 60; KG 76, 73; KG 77, 73
Kampfgruppe zum Besonderen Verwendung (KGRZBV) (Special Duties Wing): KGRZBV I and II 41, 53; KGRZBV 18, 57
Kanne, 42, 45
Keller, General Albert, 36
Kemmel, 123, 126
Kesselring, General Albert, 32, 36, 56
Kleist, General Ewald von, 33, 70, 99, 100, 109, 132, 136, 139, 142, 145
Klopfstein, 142
Kluge, General Günther von, 33, 66, 96, 145
Knokke, 61
Koblenz, 32
Koch, Captain, 41
Kortkeer River, 125
Küchler, General Georg von, 33, 59, 144

La Cassine, 86
La Chambre, Guy, 15, 16
La Galise, 149
Lackner, Colonel, 60
Landrecies, 97, 105
Langres, 64
Laon, 103, 104, 138
Leeb, General Wilhelm Ritter von, 33
Laudon valley, 139
Le Chesne, 88

Le Havre, 141, 145
Le Mans, 140
Le Quesnoy, 101, 138, 139
Leffe, 69
Lens, 120
Leopold III of Belgium : 22, 32, 128
Lepren, 91
Les Chapieux, 150
Leyden, 55
Liart, 66, 81
Libaud, General, 76
Liège, 33, 41, 48, 52, 64, 65, 66, 98
Liesse, 103
Ligny-sur-Cache, 108
Lille, 21, 27, 38
Liore et Olivier (LeO 451) bombers, 16, 36, 51, 140
List, General Sigmund Wilhelm, 33, 99, 100
Locarno, Treaty of, 2
Loddenheide, 1, 30
Loire, 144
London, 6
Longwy, 20
Lorraine, 102
Louvain, 27, 107
Luftflotte *1*, 23
   2, 1, 32, 36, 56, 59, 137
   3, 36
   4, 23
   5, 137
   Fliegerkorps : I 36; II, 36, 73; IV, 36; V, 36; VIII, 36, 73
Luftwaffe, 1, 15, 16, 29, 34, 36, 37, 47, 55, 59, 70, 72, 73, 75, 77, 78, 95, 97, 105, 106, 114, 117, 132, 137, 139, 155; *see also* Luftflotte *and* Kampfgeschwader
Lummen, 48
Luxembourg, 20, 33, 34, 46, 51, 66, 77
Lyon, 28, 81

Maaland, Liaison agent, 130
Maas River, 42, 56, 57, 58, 60, 64, 65; *see also* Meuse, River
Maastricht, 31, 43, 45, 47, 51, 56, 57, 64, 65
Machelen, 31
Madagascar, 77
Maginot, André, 21
Maginot Line, 20, 21, 26, 27, 28, 33, 64, 71, 75, 76, 142, 145
Malmy, 87
Mansell, Captain, 129
Manstein, General Erich von, 29, 30, 32, 141
Manston, Kent (RAF), 54-5
Marc, Colonel, 93
Marche, 67
Marck, R., 62
Marfée Wood, 74; *see also* Bois de la Marfée
Marioge, Colonel, 96
Marlemont, 91
Marne, River, 143
Maroeuil, 118
Maroeuil Wood, 119
Marseille, 28
Martel, Major-General, 111, 112, 113, 114, 115, 117
Martelange, 46
Martin 167 bomber, 16, 140
Martin, General, 70, 81
Matilda tanks, 35, 111, 115, 116
Mauberge, 99, 100
Mayen, 32
Mehaige, 48
Mesny, General, 101
Messerschmidts, 50, 51, 73, 79, 95, 137, 140; 108s, 1, 30, 31; 109s, 36, 37, 50; 110s, 36, 37, 54, 55
Mettet, 95
Metz, 20
Meuse River, 27, 28, 30, 33, 34, 35, 45, 48, 49, 64, 65, 67, 68, 69, 70, 71, 72, 73, 74, 75, 76, 77, 79, 80, 81, 83, 86, 87, 89, 91, 92, 95, 98, 116, 142; *see also* Maas River
Mézières, 27, 64, 65, 71, 90, 91
Moerdijk bridge, 56, 67, 58, 62

Moeres, 127, 128, 129
Molinié, General, 133
Molotov, Vyacheslav, 18
Mont-Cenis, 149
Mont St Eloi, 118
Montcornet, 81, 103
Monthermé, 33, 71, 76, 79, 83, 86, 91, 92
Montleban, 66
Montmedy, 142
Morane 406s, 36
Moravia, 12, 16
Morel, Colonel, 153
Morville, 84
Moscow, 12
Most, Lieutenant, 114, 115
Moy, 105
Munich Agreement, 2, 10, 11, 12, 16
Munster, 1; Muster-Loddenheide airfield, 1
Mureaux, 88, 115
Mussolini, Benito, 10, 146, 149, 154

Namsos, 38
Namur, 27, 50, 64, 65, 66, 70, 100
Nancy, 20
Narvik, 38
Nazis, 6, 11, 12, 133
Nazi-Soviet Non-Aggression Pact, 18
Netherlands Army Aviation, 54
Neufchâteau, 34, 46, 47
Neufchâtel, 142
Neuville St Vaast, 119
Nicholson, Brigadier, 134
Nieuport, 126
Nieuwe Maas, 57
Nijmegen, 65
Nives, 46
'Niwi' Operation, 46
Noordwijk, 55
Nordschote, 126
Normandy, 138
North Africa, 145, 154
North African units, 24, 25, 144

Norway, 38, 39
Nuremburg, 6
Nuttall, Second Lieutenant, 130

Ohrenthal Salient, 25
Oise, 93, 94, 95, 98, 102, 103, 143
Omicourt, 76
Omont, 87
Onhaye, 82
Operation Dynamo, 121, 131, 134
Operation Niwi, 46
Operation Paula, 137
Orly, General, 149
Ostheim, 41, 43
Ourthe River, 48, 67
Ovide, Corporal Blanc, 151

Panzers : see German Army
Paris, 34, 135, 137, 143, 144, 145, 146
Paris Peace Conference, 4
Pegler, Major (RE), 130
Pendred, Second Lieutenant, 131
Péronne, 105, 136, 140, 143
Perwez, 49
Pétain, Marshal, 146
Petit-Saint-Bernard, 149, 152
Petite-Gette, 48
Petre, Major-General R. L., 110
'Petreforce', 110, 120
Phillipeville, 82, 83, 84
Picquigny, 106
Plan D, see Dyle Plan
Playfair, Air Vice-Marshal, 79
Ploegsteert Château, 122
Plouvain, 118
Poland, 11, 16, 17, 22, 23, 28, 29
Polish corridor, 18
Polish fighter group, 25
Poperinghe, 123, 126, 128
Popular front in France, 14, 15
Prague, 2, 6, 16
Pratt, Brigadier Douglas, 111, 115-16
Préclaire, Colonel, 90

Pretelat, General A. G., 25
Prioux, General René-Jacques-Adolphe, 48, 49, 80, 111, 112, 113, 117, 119
Propaganda Ministry of Goebbels, 5

Quigg, Lance-Corporal, MM, 120

Raches, 119
Raeder, Admiral Erich, 9
reconnaissance troops, 28
Red Army, 18
Reich, Third, 2, 3
Reichenau, General Walter von, 33, 57, 80, 123
Reims, 88, 92, 103
Reinberger, Major Hellmuth, 1, 2, 30, 31, 32
Reinhardt, General Georg-Hans, 71, 76, 77, 98, 102, 132
Renault R.35 infantry support tanks, 13, 24, FTS, 24
Revigny, 94
Reynaud, Paul, 146
Rhine River, 7, 25, 28, 30, 41, 43, 56, 62
Rhineland, 2, 12, 20, 22, 39
Rhône River, 28
Ribbentrop, Joachim von, 18
Ribemont, 102
Richthofen, General Wolfram von, 36
Rochard, General, 71, 72
Rocroi, 91, 92
Roeux, 118
Rommel, General Erwin, 67, 79, 81, 82, 83, 95, 96, 97, 110, 114, 115, 116, 139, 140, 141, 145, 155, 156
Rothenburg General, 110
Rotterdam, 52, 56, 57, 58, 62
Roucard, General, 89
Rouen, 135, 140, 141, 143
Royal Air Force: no. 2 Group, 51, 80; Bomber Command, 37, 51, 146;

Blenheim squadrons:
  no. 12, 51, 80
  no. 15, 55
  no. 40, 55
  no. 114, 51, 80
  no. 139, 51, 80
  no. 600, 54
Fairey squadrons:
  no. 103, 79, 80
  no. 150, 79, 80
  other squadrons: nos 88, 105, 142, 218, 226, *see also* British Air Forces in France
RAF Wyton, 55
Roye, 102
Rumania, 11, 17, 18
Rumigny, 66, 92
Runciman, Walter, 1st Viscount, 6
Rundstedt, General Gerd von, 29, 33, 99, 100, 132, 134, 143
Russia, *see* USSR
Russo-Polish War, 1920, 18
Ruthenians, in Czechoslovakia, 4

Saar River, 25, 26, 28, 37
Saarbrücken, 25
Saigneville, 135
Saint Aignan, 86, 87
Saint Bernard, 153
St Catherine, 120
St Dizier, 145
St Eloi-Warneton road, 123, 124
Sainte-Foy, 150, 153
St François crossroads, 130
Saint-Mihiel, 64
St Pol, 27
Saint Quentin, 98, 103, 109
St Trond, 52
St Vaast, 118
St Valery-en-Caux, 141
St Valery-sur-Somme, 105, 106, 135
Sambre-Oise Canal, 94, 97, 98, 99, 100
Samoussy, 104
Sarraut, Albert, 2

Sarre River, 25
Savoie, 28, 148
Saxony, 5
Scarpe River, 102, 110, 112, 113, 116, 117
Scharoo, Colonel, 58, 59
Scheldt, River, 61, 62
Schiphol, 53
Schlieffen, Count von, 26
Schlieffen Plan, 21, 28, 29
Schmidt, General Rudolf, 58, 59
Schneider-Creusot works, 13
'Schwerpunkt', 32, 33
Sciard, General, 61
Seclin, 110
Sedan, 27, 30, 32, 33, 34, 46, 64, 65, 70, 71, 72, 73, 74, 76, 79, 80, 81, 86, 87, 90
Seine River, 140, 141, 144, 146
Selestat, 25, 28
Seloges, 151
Semois River, 34, 74, 77
Senne River, 107, 108, 109
Sensée, 102
Senuc, 88
Serre River, 104
'Sichelschnitt', 33, 34
Siegfried line, the, 22, 25
Signy L'Abbaye, 91
Sillery, 88
Singly, 87
Sirovy, General Jan, 10
Sissonne, 66, 104
Sivry, 97
Skoda arms complex, 9, 35
Slovakia, 12, 16, 17
Smigly-Ridz, Marshal Edouard, 18
Société d'Outillage Mecanique et d'Usinage d'Artillerie of St Ouen, 13
Soissons, 93
Solre-le-Château, 85, 97
Somme River, 105, 110, 111, 121, 132, 133, 136, 138
Somua 20 ton tank, 13, 24; cavalry tank, 36, 104
Souchez, 120

South Beveland, 61, 62, 63
Soviet Union, see USSR
Sperrle, General Hugo, 36
Sponeck, Lieutenant-General Graf, 55, 56
Stalin, Joseph, 12
Stave, 83
'Steel' Assault Detachment, 42-3
Stenay, 64
Stettin, 30
Stonne, 89, 90
Stopford, Brigadier, 119, 123
Storchs, 45, 46
Strasbourg, 25
Student, General Kurt, 57
Stuka-Geschwader, 1, 23, 77
11, 45, 73, 77
Stukas, 36, 78, 104, 108
Sudeten German Party, 4
Sudeten Germans, 4, 5, 6, 7
Sudetenland, 7, 10, 42
Switzerland, borders, 20, 28, 33

Tanks, 13; German mark 1s, 11s, 111s, 35; Mark 1vs, 35, 36, 119; see also specific types: Renault, Hotchkiss, B, B.1, D.1, D.2 etc.
Tannay, 89
Tarentaise, 149, 150
Termignon, 149
Terneuzen, 61
Tête de Bellaval, 150
Third French Republic, 14
Third Reich, 2, 3, 11
Tilburg, 61
Tirlemont, 48, 49
Tongeren, 47, 48, 51
Touchon, General, 92, 93, 94
Tours, 144, 146
Tourteron, 88
Tremblois, 92
Trois Bois, 127
Turkey, 18
Turnhout, 27

USSR, 4, 11, 12, 156

Valenciennes, 21, 101, 102
Valkenburg, 54
Vallée des Contamines, 150
Vallée des Glaciers, 150
Vauthier, General, 70
Veiel, General, 99, 100
Veldwezelt, 42, 45
Vence valley, 94
Vendresse, 76
Venlo, 65
Verdun, 19, 40, 64, 136, 145
Versailles, Treaty of, 2, 20
Vervins, 69, 80, 98
Victoria Cross, 51
Villars-sur-Bar, 76
Ville aux Bois, 103
Vimy, 27, 120
Vimy Ridge, 110, 111, 112, 118
Vining, Major, 119
Vireux, 70, 76
Vireux-Molhain, 66
Vistula River, 23
Voroshilov, Marshal Kliment von, 17
Vouzier, 70
Vraux, 51
Vroenhoven, 42, 45
Vuillemin, General Joseph, 15, 16

Waalhaven, 52, 53, 54, 55, 57
Wadelincourt, 74, 75, 89
Wailly, 115
Walcheren Island, 61, 62, 63
Walsoorden, 61, 62
War Directive No. 1, (Hitler), 23
Waremme, 47
Warndt Forest, 25
Warsaw, 18
Warsaw Pact, 157
Waterloo, 108

Wavre, 27, 49, 107
Wavrin, 38
Wehrmacht: occupation of Rhineland, 2, 12; invasion of Czechoslovakia, 5, 10; numerically inferior to allies, 22; and '*Fall Gelb*', 30, 32; and '*Sichelschnitt*', 34; armour of, 35; invasion of Low Countries, 41, 43, 44, 107, 136; *see also* German Army
Wenck, Major, 100
Wenzel, Sergeant, 45
Werner, Colonel, 67, 68
Westland Lysander, 37
Westmoerhoek, 129
Weygand, General Maxime, 13, 14, 114, 144, 146, 147
Weygand line, 136, 139
Wietersheim, General Gustav von, 33
Wilby, Second Lieutenant, 131
Wilhelmshaven, 52
Willems Bridge, Rotterdam, 57, 58, 59
Wilson, Sir Horace, 10
Witry, 46
Witzig, Lieutenant Rudolf, 42-3, 44, 45
Woensdrecht, 62
Wytschaete Ridge, 125

Ypenberg, 53, 54, 55
Ypres-Comines Canal, 122, 125, 126, 127, 155
Ypres, 114, 122, 124, 128
Yser River, 126
Yugoslavia, 11
Yvoir, 67, 68, 81

Zillebeke, 122, 123, 124